WHAT MY MOTHER GAVE ME

Also by ELIZABETH BENEDICT

Novels
Slow Dancing
The Beginner's Book of Dreams
Safe Conduct
Almost
The Practice of Deceit

Nonfiction
The Joy of Writing Sex: A Guide for Fiction Writers
*Mentors, Muses & Monsters: 30 Writers on the People Who
Changed Their Lives,* Editor

What My Mother Gave Me

Thirty-one Women on the Gifts That Mattered Most

Edited by
ELIZABETH BENEDICT

ALGONQUIN BOOKS OF CHAPEL HILL   2013

Published by
Algonquin Books of Chapel Hill
Post Office Box 2225
Chapel Hill, North Carolina 27515-2225

a division of
Workman Publishing
225 Varick Street
New York, New York 10014

Library of Congress Cataloging-in-Publication Data
What My Mother Gave Me : Thirty-one Women on the Gifts That
Mattered Most / Edited by Elizabeth Benedict.—First Edition.
pages cm
ISBN 978-1-61620-135-7
1. Mothers and daughters.   2. Parent and adult child.   3. Gifts—
Social aspects.   I. Benedict, Elizabeth, editor of compilation.
HQ755.86.W53 2013
306.874'3—dc23   2012040939

10 9 8 7 6 5 4 3 2 1
First Edition

Contents

Introduction

It is said that all books begin with an obsession, and this one is no exception.

In this case, it's a beautiful winter scarf my mother gave me toward the end of her life, probably the last gift I got from her. After she died in 2004, I became more attached to it. The times I thought I'd lost it, I went into full-blown panics. It was only partly that I didn't know where to find a replacement for this embroidered wool scarf whose label said MADE IN INDIA. Mostly, it was feeling that I'd lost my connection to my mother — a connection that was restored as soon as I found it.

The intensity of my feelings about the scarf surprised me, because I had felt so distant from my mother for most of my life. But because she was kind, loving, and needy, my feelings for her were layered with guilt, and the guilt so thick it sometimes felt like torment. After she died, I just felt sad and intensely aware of the scarf, which I wear around the collar of my coat all winter long, every year.

I lived silently with this welter of feelings year after year. I didn't know whom to talk to about it, or what to say; the scarf was attached to a free-floating, inchoate grief. Or was it something other than grief? For years, the feelings were beyond any words that I could summon. In 2011, my brooding gave way to curiosity, and I began to wonder about the experience of other women. If this one gift meant so much to me, if it unlocked the door to so much history and such complicated feelings, might other women have such a gift themselves?

What My Mother Gave Me is the affirmative answer to that question. Each of the contributors describes a gift from her mother — three-dimensional, experiential, a work habit, a habit of being, a way of seeing the world — that magically, movingly reveals the story of her mother and of their relationship. The pieces run from short and sweet to long and wrenching, from hilarious to mournful, from heartwarming to heartbreaking. And the treasured gifts shimmer in their variety and uniqueness: an etiquette book, a plant, a necklace, a horse, a passport, a trip on the Circle Line boat around Manhattan. One woman received from her writer mother the habits of writing a thousand words a day plus one charming note. Another got the gift of taking the impossible in stride. And one was given a few bottles of nail polish that changed her life.

Singly, each piece is a gem to me: a gathering in of memory, affection, and gratitude, however tormented the relationships once were. Taken together, the pieces have a force that feels as elemental as the tides: outpourings of lightness and darkness; simple joy and devastating grief; mother love and daughter love; mother love and daughter rage; the anguish of suffering mothers and daughters powerless to help them—and the spoken and unspoken weight of missing all the mothers who are gone.

Having had an unhappy mother, I found myself astonished—feeling a mixture of envy and disbelief—by the stories of happy mothers and daughters. At first, I thought it was the younger writers whose mothers were happy, those whose mothers had more control over their lives and their finances than women of my mother's generation. But as essays arrived over a period of months, I saw I was wrong: there are happy mothers from all generations in this collection. Such mothers—it's clear from these pages—raise more lighthearted offspring than unhappy ones; or do I mean only that the absence of torment is palpable in their pages?

As essay after essay reveals, a single gift can easily tell the story of an entire life. Yet for all the richness here, it's striking how modest almost all of these gifts are. A used cake pan, a homemade quilt, a wok, a Mexican blouse, a family photograph. It just might be, after all, that it's the thought that counts—and the packaging, too. I don't mean the paper and the ribbons, but the emotional wrapping, the occasion for the gift, the spirit in which it was given, and everything that happened before and after. This is another way of saying that, as gift givers and recipients—whether we are mothers, daughters, aunts, sisters, or cherished friends—we may not know for quite some time which presents will matter most.

WHAT MY MOTHER GAVE ME

Heart's Desire

· ·

ROXANA ROBINSON

Growing up, I was horse-crazy.

I thought about little else.

At school, I drew pictures of horses and wrote stories about them. At recess we all played horses, all the girls in second grade. Each day we described ourselves: "I'm a mischievous bay filly with a white star on my nose." "I'm a curvetting chestnut mare with four white socks." Then we trotted off, tossing our heads.

When I was in the car with my parents, I looked out the window and imagined myself racing alongside on horseback, keeping up with the car as I jumped over fences and obstacles. I imagined myself the rider and I imagined myself the horse: I watched for good pasture; thick, juicy green grass looked delicious to me. I watched for horse barns and riding rings. When I saw a horse in a field, I waved, covertly.

No one else in my family was so afflicted. My mother had ridden, as a girl, but she hadn't been horse-crazy. My father's father had been a polo player and foxhunter, but my own father had never taken up riding. My brothers and sisters weren't interested in horses. It was only me.

I was besotted. I had a map of the world showing the breeds and their origins. I knew that Przewalski's Horse came from Mongolia. I knew it was the oldest known breed, endearingly big-bellied and short-legged, dun-colored, with a thick black mane and tail, and no forelock. I knew the sturdy Norwegian Fjord Horse, and the American Trotting Horse, descended from Rysdyk's Hambletonian. I knew the heavy draft breeds, the huge gentle Clydesdale, the thick-necked Shire, the Suffolk Punch. I knew the Thoroughbreds, who were all descended from three Arabian foundation sires: the Godolphin Barb, the Darley Arabian, and the Byerly Turk.

I especially loved Arabians, with their delicate bones and dished faces and arched necks, their fiery natures and flowing tails. Swift and sure-footed, they galloped across the burning sands under an azure sky. They were romantic heroes, and besides, I was related to them.

The Godolphin Barb was a small Arabian stallion given as a present by the Bey of Tunis to the king of France. Somehow the little Barb (a horse from the Barbary Coast) wound up in

England, owned by the Earl of Godolphin, who had a famous racing stud. At that time, the early eighteenth century, English racehorses were big and heavy-boned. The slight, light-boned Arab—only fifteen hands high—was not considered suitable breeding stock. But the Barb was high-spirited and fiery, and more forceful than anyone expected.

A well-bred brood mare at the stud was meant to be bred to a big stallion called Hobgoblin. But the mare refused him, decisively: she preferred the Barb, and finally she was allowed to accept his advances. Their first foal, a colt called Lath, won the Queen's Plate nine times, and so began the Barb's history as one of the greatest racing sires of all time. His offspring were phenomenal runners; one of his descendants was Seabiscuit.

The name of the mare was Lady Roxana.

This was my tribe.

I read every horse book in the school library. I saved my allowance to buy my own horse books. The stories usually began with a young girl who longed for a horse, and finished with her owning one: *National Velvet, Silver Snaffles, A Pony for Jean, The Ten-Pound Pony, The Horse of Hurricane Hill, Tam the Untamed.*

In these stories the horses were bold and loving companions. They were strong and powerful, beautiful and fleet, partners in a romantic narrative. They allowed girls to enter a story about achievement. On horseback, heroines could gallop across the countryside, save people from fires and floods, leap enormous obstacles, win races, capture burglars or dognappers, raise money for a raffle, teach someone to be brave, do whatever needed to be done.

Horse books were girls' versions of superhero comics, horses our source of superpowers. And a horse offered more than a mere physical transformation; a horse offered an emotional bond. A horse was your trusted friend, your beloved companion, as well as the source of your powers.

When I was ten years old, we moved to a house with a small barn. The barn was a long building with a two-car garage in front and a roomy two-stall stable behind. Outside this was a small fenced field. It was all waiting for a horse.

We lived out in the country, and I was like a horse-seeking missile. I knew every horse for miles around, and I rode as many of them as I could. Anyone who owned one found me hanging around the barn, skinny and hopeful, in my scuffed thrift-shop boots. I went anywhere there were horses, and finally I found my own.

I had persuaded my mother to take me to a local horse show, where I spent the day staring and yearning. In the afternoon I noticed a dark-eyed boy, slightly older than me, struggling with his horse. He was holding it by the reins, trying to keep it from grazing on the lawn, and at the same time trying to get something from his trailer. I offered my services and he handed me the reins. The horse went on trying to graze, snatching greedily at the grass, her bit jingling. I fell in love. When the boy came back, I told him she was beautiful. He told me she was for sale.

Our families gathered for a meeting at the boy's house. The boy's name was Jeff. His father was handsome in a dark leathery way, and his mother was tanned and glamorous, with a ragged blond ponytail, a white sundress, and worn red leather mules. Jeff was handsome, too, with dark soulful eyes, but he was pigeon-toed.

The price of the horse was $250. His father told Jeff he'd forgive him a debt if Jeff dropped it to $200. (I was amazed that you could owe money to your parents.) My parents had told me at home that I could pay for half with the small inheritance I'd received from my grandmother and that they would pay the other half. It all depended on Jeff dropping the price to $200. Everyone in the room looked at Jeff. He nodded solemnly at his father, and Blakewell Babe was mine. My mother smiled at me.

I was twelve years old.

This was all my mother's idea, I knew.

My mother believed that every child should receive a heart's desire. She called it that, a heart's desire. She believed that children were driven by deep yearnings, and that those should, if possible, be satisfied. My older brother loved trains, and his heart's desire was to ride them, anywhere, everywhere, across the country. My parents let him. He was nine when he took his first long-distance train trip. He charted it carefully beforehand, with maps and timetables, and never missed a connection.

My mother was small and compact, with fine dark hair, aquiline features, and a square beautiful face. She had a generous heart, and she believed in taking children seriously. When she was three years old she had polio, and for a time she was paralyzed from the waist down. She recovered, mostly, though for the rest of her life her legs and feet were troublesome. She never let this slow her down, though. She played tennis, and danced, and climbed mountains, and traveled, and had five children, and lived the life she wanted to live. But I think the polio made her particularly attentive to the dreams of children. I think she remembered not being able to walk.

That day, after the meeting, I rode my horse back home, cross-country, clopping quietly along the roads and the edges of fields and finally turning up our gravel driveway and into the wide pasture gate. I had a horse of my own.

Blakewell Babe was a small red chestnut mare, about fifteen hands high. She was a purebred American Saddle Horse; I was proud of her breeding, and I still have her papers somewhere. She was short-legged and straight-necked, not much of a beauty, but she was good-tempered and willing, and I loved her. She became the center of my life.

At feeding time I taught her to pick me up. She came down from the barn to where I sat on the fence by the house. She sidled sideways so I could jump easily aboard, then carried me up to the barn. Inside, she took me to the ladder leading to the hayloft. I climbed up it to pour grain into her bucket, drop hay into the stall. Sometimes I sat on her back while she ate her hay. Not while she ate grain — then she was testy, and might lay back her ears at me. But while she ate hay she was quiet and peaceful, and I could sit on her. I liked the steady sound she made, and the smells of sweet hay and clean horse.

I never learned to ride properly — I didn't take many lessons. But I didn't care about this: most of my riding took place in a wild romantic dream. I liked riding bareback, because that seemed most authentic. *She was one with her horse,* I would think. I learned to jump bareback, starting a lifetime of bad riding habits. (To this day I can't seem to put my weight in my stirrups, which means I am hopeless at dressage.) I rode badly but everywhere.

We jumped chicken coops and split-rail fences, we scrambled up banks and across creeks. We trotted on winding trails through the woods, we cantered through open fields. We galloped at full speed up dirt roads, Babe's ears flattened, her hoofs beating out a hard clattery tattoo, her long red tail streaming behind.

I fell off a zillion times. I was bucked off, or I slid off over her head when she put it down suddenly, or I was jolted off over a jump. The first time I jumped bareback I fell off and had to have four stitches under my chin. The day of my first date I fell off and broke my pelvis, and spent the next six weeks flat on my back.

In the spring I rode bareback, with a halter and lead shank, out into a neighbor's field, where the grass was thick and juicy. I sat on her back while she grazed. She took one slow step after another, her head moving in a tugging semicircle as she reached for the new grass. Sometimes I sat backwards, brushing her smooth back. Sometimes I lay on her, my arms hanging down on either side. Her beautiful body was my landscape. It was the place I knew best: its smell, its shape, its textures. The moleskin softness of her muzzle, her loose muscular lips, the polished summer smoothness of her chestnut flanks. The sweet grassy scent of her breath, the deep calm of her sigh. The beautiful liquid darkness of her eyes.

In the barn I was on my own. I learned everything myself: how to get the bit into a horse's mouth on a cold day (warm it first in your hand), or what to do if the frog (the soft part of her hoof) turned mushy and foul (it was a fungus called thrush, and you painted it with gentian violet). I learned how to clean tack, and when to call the vet and the blacksmith; I learned the sweet charring smell of the forge. I learned from books, or from watching other people.

I didn't mind doing any of this alone. I remembered that day at the family meeting, my mother's smile of trust and complicity, and her certainty. She'd given me a whole world, and she trusted me to enter into it. Looking back, I'm amazed that she had so much confidence, that she felt so certain that a twelve-year-old girl could look after a horse. But she did.

I think this had to do with her generosity, her willingness to believe in other people and let them go their own ways. She believed in independence, and she trusted people. She trusted them to do the right thing, whatever that meant. She rarely criticized anyone; she believed in seeing the best in them. Growing up as her daughter, that felt like a gift.

In tenth grade I went away to boarding school; my parents took care of Babe. It wasn't so much work, after all, if you weren't horse-crazy. She was never shut inside her stall, she wandered in and out at will, so there wasn't much cleaning to do, only the daily feedings. Whenever I came home I took charge again, going out to the barn to feed and brush and ride her, arranging for whatever she needed. When I called home I always asked about her. "Babe is fine," my mother always said, and gave me the news: she'd grown a thick winter coat, or she'd just been shod. In the winter she took to lying peacefully in the pasture, curling up like a dog in front of the barn, where the warmth was reflected off the walls.

After that I never lived at home again. I went on to college, then to other things. Who comes back to live at home once you've left?

I always asked about her, but over the years I stopped riding her when I came home. She was too shaggy, the saddle was too dry, my interests were elsewhere. But still I never wanted to sell my horse, and my parents never asked me to. She had been my heart's desire. She would always be at the center of that romantic passage in my life, when she was my partner in the wild, dangerous, and beautiful ride across adolescence.

My horse stayed on, growing old and stiff, ambling quietly about our small pasture, dozing in the sun. She died at the age of thirty-one, which is ninety-three in horse years. It was my mother who found her, one day in early March, stretched out in the muddy field.

The Missing Photograph

CAROLINE LEAVITT

When I was growing up in Boston in the 1960s, my life was awash in flashbulbs. My older sister, Ruth, and I could be romping wildly around the living room, dancing to the soundtrack of *West Side Story,* and before you could say Leonard Bernstein, my mother would have snapped a dozen shots of us with her Brownie camera. We blinked at the sudden shock of light, but we always willingly posed, our hands behind our heads, our toes artfully pointed. We were little hams. "Wait! Wait! Take one more!" we begged, and she did.

There were pictures of us festooned all over our house. On the walls and in photo albums, stuffed in boxes and on top of everyone's dresser. My mother was our own personal Stieglitz, documenting our lives so precisely that she carefully labeled every photo, both by year and by event. We took pictures, too, of our cat, Elvis, and of each other, but it never dawned on me until I was twelve that there were no photos of my mother anywhere in the house, not even of her as a child. It made sense to us that there wouldn't be photos of her and our father, since he was seldom home, and when he was, he was silent and sulky or arguing with all of us. Their wedding photos were stuck in a white plastic album, and we had the same relationship to them as we did with our father: we didn't want to get too close to them. Our mother didn't like posing along with us, her two girls, and we couldn't understand it. She was beautiful and she could never pass a mirror without looking into it, fluffing her hair or fixing her collar, but she still didn't want her image captured. "I take terrible pictures," she insisted. "I'm too old to be photographed."

"But what about when you were our age?" I asked. "You probably took great pictures then! Where are the pictures of you as a little girl?"

My mother came from a family of eight siblings and two Russian immigrant parents who both escaped the czar, a life that seemed so far away from Waltham, so exotic, that we were dying to see the proof of it, but even our aunts and uncles didn't have photos. "No one really took photographs," my mother told me. "Your father doesn't have any of him as a kid, either. It was just different. Not many people took pictures back then and we didn't have these fancy flash cameras."

"Didn't that make you mad?" we wanted to know. "Didn't you want pictures?"

My mother shrugged. "Well," she said finally, "there was one picture taken when I was twelve, but it was of my whole family, and I have no idea where it is."

She had that look on her face she always had when she was hiding information from us. She wouldn't meet our eyes. She pursed her lips. We didn't believe her. We searched our basement, turning up old dolls, worn stuffed animals, and boxes of our own artwork and school papers. At family gatherings, we begged our aunts and uncles, "Who has the photo?" They looked at us as if we'd asked who knew how to do open-heart surgery. No one, it seemed, knew where that photo was or thought it was important.

"Tell us what you looked like," I begged my mother.

"I don't remember."

"Did you have curls? Were you fat or thin?"

She laughed and told me how much fun it was to grow up in a big family with so many sisters and brothers. What a gift it was! How lucky she had been! She told us how her father, an Orthodox rabbi, always had the whole congregation over to dinner every week and how everyone sang and danced, beating a rhythm with real silver spoons on my grandmother's polished wood table. She mentioned how her sisters saved their most beautiful clothes for her, handing down velvet dresses and watered silk shirts, how they fussed over her because she was the baby. "Family is everything," my mother insisted. "You girls remember that." As if to prove it, she still lived within twenty minutes of all of her sisters, and they were always at the house, a trail of exotic names like Freda, Theodora, Gertrude, and the more American Jean, and if they argued sometimes, I told myself, well, I argued with my own sister, and I still adored her. Arguments didn't have to mean that there wasn't love.

As I got older, I couldn't stop thinking about the missing photograph and wondering what it would tell me about my mother. I wanted it to reveal that she was the prettiest of all her sisters, that she had the most personality. I wanted the picture to show me who my mother was before my father fell in love with her and then changed his mind and grew cruel. My sister and I hit adolescence, and suddenly my mother, who was always fussing about her own appearance, saw our pain. My sister came home crying because two girls at school had mocked her awkward pixie haircut. Our mother immediately took my sister to John Robert Powers Modeling Agency and they gave her a makeover, telling her she had the wrong clothes and the wrong hairdo, something my mother rectified with a flash of her credit card and two trips to Clip 'N' Curl in Belmont and to Filene's in downtown Boston. When a boy in my history class drew a caricature of me on the blackboard, all medusa-haired and skinny, I came home and tried, secretively, to iron my curly hair straight. I broke the iron and singed my hair, and had to admit both matters to my mother. She put her arms around me and then she took me to the Star Market to get a box of Curl Free.

But my sister and I were still sensitive about our looks. We didn't want our images caught on film anymore. We put our hands up when our mother approached with the camera. "Now that makes me very sad," our mother said, but we were teenagers, and we didn't care about making anyone happy but ourselves.

We grew up. Our father died the year I graduated college and we hoped our mother would remarry, choosing a kind, funny man this time, getting the second chance at love we thought she deserved, but she seemed uninterested in meeting anyone. We got married ourselves and moved away, and there were oceans of photographs documenting our lives. After I gave birth to my son, and my husband and I began capturing his life in pictures and videos, I began to think about that missing photo again. It became a missing link in this whole chain of glorious family. I couldn't go home to see my family without asking where it was.

"What does it matter?" my mother said. "It's just an old photo."

By the time my son was twelve, almost all of my mother's family had died. Then my aunt Jean passed on, and my mother called, not just to tell me about her sister's death, but to say, her voice strained, "I found the photo in Jean's basement." I imagined her voice sounded funny because of her sister's death, because of her grief. I told myself that when I got home, I would make her feel better. *Imagine that,* I thought, *a whole family, except for my mother, gone, but the photo has suddenly appeared.*

My sister and I traveled back to Boston for my aunt Jean's funeral and to see my grieving mother and the photo. We sat in our living room, all three of us on the floral couch, our bare feet sinking into our mother's blue wall-to-wall carpeting. "Ready?" our mother said. She had a box on her lap and she opened it, slowly taking the photo out and handing it to us, almost shyly. I gasped but my sister was silent, as transfixed as I was. The photo was bigger than I thought it would be—eight by twelve—and it was sepia toned. Everyone was standing: my Russian grandmother, who always terrified me, was in a floor-length velvet dress, one hand balanced on my Orthodox rabbi grandfather's shoulder as if she were pressing him into his chair. My aunts, in flapper dresses and boyish bobs, were so young and happy beside my three preening uncles, one even wearing thick, tweedy knickers. Which one was my mother? Surely not the small girl, like a brown wren, hidden in the corner like an afterthought. I looked again. This girl was younger than all the others, in a misshapen dress, in dirty knee socks, her hair raggedly cut, looking as if she would smile if she wasn't about to burst into tears.

My mother, sitting between us, tapped the girl who was so out of place she might belong to another family. "There I am," she said. Her voice slowed. "Don't I look so homely." She said it as if it were a fact.

Shocked, I stared at the photograph. Surely that couldn't be her. I felt a flash of shame for her, and then guilt that I had badgered her about this photograph for so many years, and all I had to do was look at that little girl to know why she hadn't wanted me to see it. I looked closer, and suddenly I couldn't take my eyes off her as a child.

"You look like the most interesting one there," I decided, and it was true. The others looked like they'd be happy-go-lucky guests at a party, but this stormy-eyed little girl—well, she'd have a story to tell and you'd have to listen to it.

"Really? You think so?" my mother said. She looked at me doubtfully. "No one else in my family thought so."

"But I thought your family life was so wonderful," my sister said, and my mother sighed.

"It wasn't," she said abruptly, and it was as if a closed door had swung open.

"Tell us," I said. She hesitated and slowly began. It was like a movie reel unspooling in front of us, with a plot and characters we always thought we knew.

She was a twin—which she had never told us—and one night, when she was eight, her mother had presented her and her brother to company. "Isn't the boy handsome!" my grandmother said. "And smart, too!" My mother stood, rocking from foot to foot, waiting, but no praise or attention came her way.

"Oh, and here's the girl," my grandmother said offhandedly, and then she dismissed the twins to attend to her guests.

"But that's awful!" my sister said.

"I was the runt of the litter," my mother said. "I had terrible teeth and my parents wouldn't send me to the dentist. I had to pay for my braces myself when I was older, and thank God I found a sympathetic dentist who let me pay over time." Her sisters, except for Jean, ignored her. The gorgeous hand-me-downs she had told us about were really worn at the elbows and ragged at the hems. We were always proud that our mom had gone to college to be a teacher, the only one of her sisters to do so, but now she told us the truth. "My parents were afraid no one would ever want to marry me, and I needed to be able to support myself because they weren't going to do it. I didn't really want to go." Even more horrifying, her father had urged her to go to an adult camp in New Hampshire to find a mate, and when she had met my father, a silent, surly brute she didn't really love, she had felt pressured into marrying him because her sisters had kept telling her, "Who else will marry you?"

Sitting beside her on the couch, I was heartbroken for my mother and I began to see all the dating advice she had ever given me through a different lens. Look for kindness. Don't settle. Look deeper than outward appearances.

"Your family was awful," I announced. It all made sense to me now, the way my mother would sometimes snap at one of her sisters when they told her what to do, and we wouldn't understand why. I pointed out how beautiful she was back then, and my mother looked at me, startled. She said when she was a newlywed and she and our father were looking for a house of their own, which she was looking forward to, our aunt Freda had browbeat her into moving into our grandmother's house instead. "You'll save money," Freda had insisted, "and you can keep an eye on our mother." It would be years before our parents moved out, years before my mother understood that she had been manipulated into taking on the job that no one else wanted and that had robbed her of privacy and a home of her own.

She told us how she had stayed married to our father, on the rebound from a man she loved, because she didn't feel that she deserved any better. She admitted that when my father died, he had left her no life insurance and that her sisters, who lived ten minutes away, didn't come over to the house to help or comfort her. "Well, it's not as if it was a great love," her sister Gertrude told her. "You'll get over it fast."

My sister and I sat beside her until four in the morning, listening to her stories, each one sadder than the next. We asked questions, we tried to stay silent, we were busy absorbing this alternate history that was the realest story she could ever tell us. But with each story, our mother seemed to be getting lighter. She seemed to be growing more beautiful. The girl in the photograph was growing more lovely, too, as my mother unburdened herself.

I took the photograph onto my lap and I pointed out the things she wasn't seeing. Her hair might be raggedly cut, but look how thick and glossy it was. The dress she was wearing might be too big for her, but get a gander at how she had rolled up the sleeves as if to give it style. "Yes, I could spiff things up," she said, and her eyes sparkled.

My sister pointed out how false a picture my mother had given us of her family life. "Why didn't you just tell us the truth?" she asked.

"I was ashamed," my mother said.

"But why?" I said. "They were the ones in the wrong, not you." I shook my head. "I love this photo," I told her. "It's you."

It made me love her more, knowing how she had struggled. It made me realize how she made a decision with her two girls, never to do what had been done to her, to make us feel special, even when we were gangly teenagers. She couldn't change her past, but she could try to change our futures with every photograph she snapped, every image of us she had proudly displayed on her walls.

A week later, as I was packing for home, my mother gave me two big brown bags of groceries—things I could buy anywhere but which she insisted I take. Boxes of pasta, jars of sauce. Green grapes I could munch on the ride home. Food, for her, was part of love. "And something else," she said and handed me the photograph.

"You don't want it?"

"I want you to have it more," she said. "Just don't forget to make a copy for your sister."

I HUNG THE photo in my office, and every day I find myself looking at it. When friends come over, they gravitate to it, studying my beautiful grandmother, my stylish young aunts, but the one they always remark on, the one small figure that catches them the most, is that haunted little girl pushed off to a corner. "That's my mom," I say.

I know what she has given me. Not just a deeper part of herself, but a part she had kept hidden that she was now giving me permission to show off. She gave me not just a photo I loved, but a message. Look deeper. Don't accept the version of the truth you were told. There are stories behind stories. The truth is always right in front of you if you are patient enough to search for it.

Mess Up Your Mind

MAUD NEWTON

At three years old and at four, my greatest desire in the world, apart from red ruffled underwear, gumball-machine emerald rings, a really nice father, and a vast cache of candy, was to read for myself, the way my parents did. All those letters arranged into all those words that filled all those books, all inaccessible to me except when someone else decoded them — it was a torment. The mysterious volumes grown-ups liked even had stories without pictures. Stories, my mother said, where your mind made its own pictures. But I would have to age into those.

I was a sheltered child, but independent. As a toddler, I insisted far too early on feeding myself. Strained turkey, beets, and carrots covered my face, spattered my clothes and high chair, and made their way under my fingernails and into my hair. My mother would carry me, still in the filthy throne, outside to be hosed down. I don't remember those disastrous feedings; I've only witnessed my mother's dramatic reenactments. Nor do I recall what she read, in the days before the Lord, but often, when she wasn't chasing after me or taking in sewing or typing for money, she begged me to be quiet and then sat alone, as long as I let her, sinking into the world of whatever book she held in her hands. After we were Saved, that book was the Bible. I remember watching her, bored and wistful, jealous of the book because it had my mother's attention and jealous of her because she knew how to disappear into the book.

She read to me, too, constantly, fluidly, dramatically — delighting with me in the stories and delighting in my delight. I remember her laughing, the warmth of her yellow eyes on mine, as we invented dialogue and subplots and worried what would happen to the characters after the last page. Insisting that we go over the same books again and again, I memorized the text, the inflections, when to turn the pages. And then I sat my mother down and "read" them to her, the tales of the very old woman and the very old man and their millions of cats, of the doctor who sailed the world with his menagerie, of the tiny duck who missed his roundup call at the fishing boat and got swatted when he caught up with it the next night. But she was quick to clarify that reciting was not reading. When I could read for myself, she said, I would understand everything differently.

SOME CHILDREN LEARN to identify words without training. But even knowing the stories by heart, running my eyes over and over them as I said the lines aloud, I lacked the cognition to make the leap. Years later I saw a movie about Helen Keller, and afterward I lay awake worrying—knowing— that if I'd been born (as we said then) deaf and dumb, I would never have experienced the eureka moment that Helen did. I would never have deduced how to read or to speak, would never have exulted with my long-suffering tutor in the hallway.

I was expected to be a prodigy of some kind. My parents had married, my mother told me, not for love but because they believed they would have smart children together. We all did our part to make this eugenics experiment a success. I attempted to use multisyllabic words in sentences. I worked my little wooden puzzles under the sofa and brought them out when complete for praise. At two and a half, I started attending a Montessori school where kids were taught to read, to the limits of their abilities, as they expressed interest, and where mothers congregated after hours in the parking lot to engage in faux-polite one-upsmanship about their child's progress vis-a-vis all the other children. My mother didn't exactly blend. In her mid-thirties, five to ten years older than the others, sole Silent Generationist in a sea of Boomers, she idolized Frank Sinatra and loathed the Beatles. She pined for the days of structured education, especially phonics, and could not hide her contempt at all the touchy-feely goings-on. Worst of all, she had arrived in South

Florida only very recently, with a thick Texan accent people had trouble understanding.

Perhaps she was embarrassed, too. Though verbally advanced and socially astute, I was tiny and sickly and incredibly clumsy, incapable of cartwheels, averse to dancing, slow in learning to do things other kids took for granted, like turning on lamps, tying shoelaces, and blowing my nose. Maybe some of my peers were also learning more quickly — I don't know. Not yet three, I was, my mother claims, showing signs that I would read soon, but my tenure at the school ended, I'm told, not long after she arrived to pick me up one day and found me and the other children acting like monkeys, ooh-ooh-oohing and leaping around. When she ordered me to stop, I pretended to be an elephant, waving my arms together like a trunk to grab her cigarette. That night my father refamiliarized my back end with his belt and it was decided that I would be removed from this hippie quagmire of permissiveness and passive-aggressive antagonism.

Conveniently, my parents had just found Jesus. So they did the natural thing; they enrolled me in the nursery school at our Presbyterian church until some more suitable situation for a Great Mind such as mine could be found. There I learned to print the letters of the alphabet. I learned to mold clay and eat paste. I learned that other children were allowed to watch a lot of television, and I learned to pretend that I watched it, too. But I did not learn to read.

When at last my mother found someone she deemed fit to educate me, someone who used the same phonetic methods, now out of fashion, by which she herself had learned, I was nearly five. I sat in a tiny room at a small table with an extremely large woman who showed me how to use a bookmark and to sound out words, and who had me memorize long lists of letter combinations and sounds—and it worked! The stories in the readers turned into stories in my mind. Soon I, like my mother, could sit with a stack of books, quietly turning pages.

Mom had majored in English literature, even gotten her master's, yet she'd settled on this course of study almost by accident. She'd entered the university as both a chemistry major and a pretty sorority girl, a mix considered by definition incompatible in the late 1950s. Ridiculed into journalism, she dropped out of that, too, after a clash with a teacher who wanted her to "write things in a certain way that didn't allow for creativity in language or approach." So she stumbled into literature and discovered (though she was intimidated by the wealthy kids who'd learned in high school how to write term papers on motif and symbolism) a native facility for critical reading. She knew characters and their motivations, and she knew—coming from a line of eccentric Texans and hillbillies, and having been raised by a hardworking, no-nonsense divorcée while her father married and divorced a string of wealthy widows and C-list starlets—how extreme and unreliable people could be, how mysterious their motivations. For a while she dabbled in philosophy, too. Ultimately, though, she blamed Sartre, Nietzsche, and their ilk for an existential crisis that led her to a psychiatrist, who told her she had mother issues.

In a different era, she might have become a writer. Instead she strived to be practical. She taught school. She managed an office at Texas Instruments and tried her hand at light computer programming. She married a gregarious, woman-izing social-climber of an attorney who didn't want kids, triangulated out of that relationship with a soul-crushing af-fair, and then married another lawyer, my father, and they embarked on their mission to breed smart children together.

This project lost focus once Mom started to interpret the Scriptures for herself. She spoke in tongues and proph-esied, and eventually started her own church. She forbade observance of Halloween, declared Santa Claus a pagan, and held her own exorcisms. At last she had justification for disapproving of rock music, which she deemed satanic and likely to result in demon possession.

Secular books should have been forbidden, too, for consis-tency's sake. The novelist Jeanette Winterson has written of being allowed only to read the Bible and six or seven other religious volumes. She actually watched as her Pentecos-tal mother threw her collection of contraband paperbacks onto a bonfire. But I was still allowed, even encouraged, to read almost any stories I chose. As long as I steered clear of magic—no *A Wrinkle in Time* for me—Mom didn't look too closely at what I picked up in thrift stores or at the library. And because I often stayed home sick, and, even more often, "sick," I spent entire weeks in bed, racing through the seven library books I was allowed to check out at a time and then nagging her into going back and checking out seven more. She did not prevent me from reading Judy Blume or Paula Danziger, or, at the age of eleven, Paul Zindel's *My Darling, My Hamburger,* a teen abortion story that still makes me flinch when I think about it.

I see now that my mother's ignorance about the books I read must have been, at some level, willful. Although she had devoted her life to God, she could not fully relinquish the smart-child experiment. She still needed me to distinguish myself in a way she herself had not been allowed to, and my increasingly undistinguished performance in math and science made clear that this would happen, if it happened at all, only through words.

Eventually my mother would excoriate my opinions and my tastes. She would accuse me of being pretentious, uppity, and condescending. She would confiscate my copies of *Nausea* and *Thus Spake Zarathustra,* warning me they'd "mess up your mind." "You'd better get right with Jesus instead of mucking around with all that pseudo-intellectual tripe," she would say, when I moved back home after college to recuperate from an illness. The implication was that my body had turned against me because I, by focusing on wicked, secular things, had turned against God.

Until then, though, her desire to acquaint me with the classics, to share the worlds her own mind had once lived in, trumped her conviction that any art not focused on God was a sin. On my fourteenth birthday, she took me to Books & Books, a beautifully curated shop in downtown Coral Gables, and filled my arms with paperbacks: *A Farewell to Arms, The Great Gatsby, East of Eden, Wuthering Heights, Jane Eyre* . . . "You're old enough to stop reading garbage now," she said. "You're old enough for these."

A Farewell to Arms may have been the first literary novel I loved. Hemingway is accused of machismo, sentimentality, blankness, and misogyny, but I didn't know about any of that then. Nor did I know anything significant about love or death or war, the central concerns of the book. The doomed romance—like crack to a teenage girl—hooked me, but it was the weird and delicate balance between detachment and intense self-awareness that drew me to the narrator.

I believed everything he said. I thought he talked just the way someone who'd lived through trauma like that would talk. The troops, the mountains, the hills, and the girls were all coolly, precisely observed. And when I got to passages like this, I scrawled them into my notebook: "We were never lonely and never afraid when we were together. I know that the night is not the same as the day: that all things are different, that the things of the night cannot be explained in the day, because they do not then exist, and the night can be a dreadful time for lonely people once their loneliness has started. But with Catherine there was almost no difference in the night except that it was an even better time. If people bring so much courage to this world the world has to kill them to break them, so of course it kills them. The world breaks every one and afterward many are strong at the broken places. But those that will not break it kills. It kills the very good and the very gentle and the very brave impartially. If you are none of these you can be sure it will kill you too but there will be no special hurry."

I remember feeling that the book was telling me something about my mother, about who she was without Jesus—lonely and anxious and prone to lying awake in the darkness—and why she felt she needed Him. Reading Hemingway, reading all these novels, made me feel closer to her than actually being with her did. They weren't just fiction, they were artifacts. They showed me who this woman—who'd once laughed with me over my storybooks, who'd stood so awkwardly with the other mothers in the school parking lot—had been before she became someone who lived for the Lord.

Still, I must have internalized my mother's discomfort with the bookish part of herself—and, by extension, her discomfort with the bookish part of me. Until a couple years ago, I secretly viewed fiction and essays as a vaguely shameful hobby. Realizing this, I stopped going out after work. I ceased reviewing. I worked on my novel for hours each day. I even started to tell my mother that I was writing. At first, she changed the subject. Not out of disapproval so much as an unease so deep-seated, so reflexive, she wasn't even aware of it. Her urge to steer the conversation elsewhere was practically Pavlovian. But I persisted, complimenting her storytelling as I did, and eventually she started to dig up old books, Hemingway and Faulkner hardcovers, and send them to me.

It must be a relief to her, knowing where those stories go, finally. And it must have given her pleasure — I know it did me — to learn that we have the same favorite novelist: that religion-obsessed master, Graham Greene.

My Disquieting Muse

. . . .

JEAN HANFF KORELITZ

In the spring of 1982, I was a twenty-year-old exchange student at Harvard, struggling in a Freud seminar so far over my head that I sometimes wondered whether the class was being conducted in German. In my downtime, I wrote poetry, which I'd been doing for years. I thought of myself as a poet, but the cold hard truth was that I hadn't read much poetry. That is, by poets who were not . . . me.

To my younger self, nothing seemed wrong with that situation. After all, I considered poetry to be all about self-expression, sort of like therapy, not to be picked apart or — *studied*. Not to be considered in relation to history or literary convention. Not to be, you know, *judged* in any way, except by how it made the reader *feel*. And if the purpose of reading other people's was to feel what they were feeling when they wrote it, well, I was a little too busy with what *I* was feeling for that sort of thing.

At the same time, I didn't allow the fact of my being poorly read to keep me off the Harvard poetry circuit. I remember arriving late to a reading by Allen Ginsberg, where the only available floor space was next to a man with a long gray ponytail, who, I would learn, was Ginsberg's lover, Peter Orlovsky. When he began rubbing some strong smelling unguent on his palms, rocking back and forth, and chanting along with the poet, I understood why everyone had given him a wide berth.

Orlovsky certainly seemed to be feeling what Ginsberg was feeling. He chimed his agreement like a congregation of one, grunting and rocking to the poet's homoerotic declarations (still just a tiny bit shocking to my twenty-year-old self) and his complaints about convention, while I leaned away from him in extreme discomfort.

Clearly, I was not bound for disembodied poetics; I was far too uptight to turn on, and too ambitious to drop out. When it came to my own poetic allegiances, Ginsberg (and Orlovsky) could probably have taken one look at me and pegged me exactly. I was adolescent (still), poetic, moody, feminist, and — it went without saying — misunderstood. It was only a matter of time before I fell beneath the sway of a certain strain of lyrical intensity, a white-hot declaration of brilliance and femaleness and power. The verse, in other words, was already on the wall.

In the dollar bin of a Harvard Square bookstore I found a paperback edition of Sylvia Plath's *Letters Home: Correspondence 1950–1963*. Those letters—I swallowed them whole: the brave soldier in her scholarship-girl dormitory, working far more diligently than I ever had (she would not have had the slightest difficulty in my Freud seminar); the breathless correspondent from the land of WASP affluence (her description of William F. Buckley Jr.'s sister's coming-out party is an astounding document of the times); the American abroad, voracious for life experiences.

The sheer force of Sylvia Plath overwhelmed me. Just imagining the energy required for her to be good at so many things made me exhausted. Her studiousness, the hours hunched over the thesaurus to produce her poetry, draft after draft of each poem, the magazine articles, the stories, even the letters themselves— often typed and running pages long—not to mention the rumored, unpublished journals. Where did she find the time? The energy? I could barely do my schoolwork and dash off a poem now and then.

Well, that semester I found the energy to read Plath. After the letters, I read her poems. I read her stories in *Johnny Panic and the Bible of Dreams,* and *The Bell Jar.* I read the first—and probably the worst—of the many inadequate biographies to come (Edward Butscher's *Sylvia Plath: Method and Madness*).

I began to assemble an idea of Plath, a composite of her art, the memories of others, and the letters, which (in that time before her journals were published) seemed to me the best available insights into her private thoughts.

I wanted very much to know what those thoughts had been.

Most likely I already knew that I wasn't alone in my fixation. I'd caught glimpses of what Anne Sexton famously called "her kind" as I went my poetic way, immersing myself in Plath's life and work. She was hardly obscure, and I was hardly the only young, sensitive, and, for that matter, angry young woman to fall beneath her spell. And though I loved her, and though my reverence for what she had accomplished was—and indeed remains—well nigh limitless, I had a sense that we admirers were probably legion. I might have begun the term as a bourgeois, poetry-writing exchange student from Dartmouth, but within weeks of encountering Plath's letters, I was heading straight for "Death Girl" territory. (The Death Girls, protagonists of Meg Wolitzer's first novel, *Sleepwalking,* published that year, were black-clad college-girl acolytes of Plath and Anne Sexton who gathered in their dorm rooms amid candlelight and cigarette smoke to read the poems and invoke the presences.)

That spring could not have been the first time I had ever experienced mild depression, but it was the first time I remember thinking of what I was feeling as depression. It was also the first time I ever romanticized depression. It was occurring to me that so many of the great writers, the ones Plath and I both admired the most, had suffered crippling mood swings and devastating sadness, not to mention actual psychosis. The tribe included not only Plath and Sexton, but Robert Lowell, their onetime teacher, and his friend John Berryman. Byron! Keats! And those were just the poets. At the end of the day, it felt as if the entire *Norton Anthology* had done time at McLean and Austin Riggs!

That semester, depression and madness were downright enthralling. I couldn't stop myself from taking constant personal inventory of my own tendencies, and wondering if every instance of Sunday morning blues might be cultivated to produce a full-blown suicidal ideation.

I didn't understand it at the time, but it's clear to me now that I was heading for a very unhappy place. I was heading there, but I never got there, because something stopped me. Something came slamming down in my path and blocked the way, as dramatically, if not as comically, as the animated foot of God descending from the cartoon clouds in the Monty Python credits.

That foot was my mother.

I turned twenty-one in May of that year, and the gift I asked her for was the newly published *Journals of Sylvia Plath*, edited by Frances McCullough with Ted Hughes consulting. Like most of Plath's admirers, I had heard about the journals, and two weeks before my birthday, on May 2, I had avidly read

Nancy Milford's review in the *New York Times Book Review*.
I couldn't wait to get my hands on the new book, so when
my mother called to ask whether there was something I especially wanted, I put in my request.

It is time, as Charles Ryder might say right around now,
to speak of my mother.

You have to understand, I was not thinking about her at
all. She was not part of the picture, that spring. The voice
in Plath's poems and her college girl novel, the voice of the
(mostly) loving daughter in the letters—that was the voice
of someone my own age, someone going to classes, mooning
over boys, worrying about whether she was good enough as
a poet and pretty enough as a woman and generally capable
of doing everything she wanted to do in life. I heard her as a
friend, as someone who would understand my own concerns
had she alighted, through a warp of time and space, beside
me in my Dunster House dormitory room. I had never con-
ceived of her as being remotely like my *mom*.

It had not dawned on me that my mother and Sylvia Plath
were almost exact contemporaries, or that the two children
left behind by Plath's suicide were almost exact contemporaries of . . . me.

I know. I know. Even all these years later, it still amazes me.

The fact was that Sylvia Plath and my mother had entered
college only a year apart—Plath at Smith, my mother at
the ultra-arty Goddard College in Vermont. Goddard was

so out-there and countercultural that when I happened to visit it years later, I immediately phoned my mother to ask, "What were you thinking?" What she was thinking was that she was going to Goddard, then an experimental, unaccredited college, because of a sculptor on its faculty named Richard Lippold, with whom her high school art teacher had suggested she study. As fate would have it, however, Lippold sold his first piece to MoMA that year, and departed Goddard with all due haste. My mother never even met him. Instead, she spent two years in northern Vermont, wearing flannel shirts and having (she assures me) a very good time, but learning absolutely nothing, until she realized that she was on track to graduate without having been educated. Then, in what may have been her first recorded act of coolheaded, world-class negotiation, she persuaded the comparatively conventional Sarah Lawrence College to accept her, in spite of an academic transcript their admissions office could not even understand, let alone evaluate. My mother proposed that the school accept her conditionally, "without status," and that if her work was sufficiently good at the end of the semester, she could be registered in the junior class; if not, they could enroll her as a sophomore and she would repeat the year. (Perhaps not quite so coolheaded, she now admits: "Also, I cried.") Sarah Lawrence said yes.

Sixty years on, my mother still admires Richard Lippold's sculptures in the atrium of Avery Fisher Hall, and dangling over the bar in the Four Seasons. Do I need to add that she never became a sculptor? She became a therapist, making it her life's work to say the right thing at the right time to any number of people as clueless as I was on the morning of my twenty-first birthday.

I remember any number of these right things. Perhaps we have time for just one more.

In 1992, when Woody Allen left Mia Farrow for her daughter Soon-Yi Previn, I was in a quandary. I *liked* Woody Allen. I liked his films, liked his way of looking at the world, and the way I sometimes saw him slouching around Manhattan, where we both lived. Most of all I liked how he loved our city, because I loved New York the same way, and when he filmed it at its most ravishing, I swooned right alongside him. When he ran off with Soon-Yi Previn, I wanted not to be furious at him, because I wanted to continue going to his films and thinking well of him. I talked this over with my mother.

"I'm sure he didn't plan for this to happen," I said to her. "You can't choose who you fall in love with. 'The heart wants what it wants' and all that," I added, quoting the man himself.

My mother regarded me with an expression of purest disgust.

"He couldn't have found . . . *another* . . . nineteen-year-old girl?" she said.

It hit me like a ton of bricks on a freight train. Oh my

God. She was totally, totally right. The man was scum, utter, thorough scum. What the hell was he doing, sleeping with his partner's daughter, or his stepdaughter, or whatever she was to him? Did it matter what she was to him? She was something to him that *you do not sleep with*. That was twenty years ago, and I have never paid money to see a Woody Allen film since.

But I digress.

On my twenty-first birthday, my mother came to celebrate with me in Cambridge, and presented me with the brand new *Journals of Sylvia Plath*. I still remember my first sight of it, the shiny lilac damask cover that has now spent thirty years on my bookshelves, in every place I've lived since then: Cambridge, Massachusetts; Cambridge, England; Ireland; New York; Massachusetts; and now Princeton, New Jersey. I wanted to start reading it right away.

But then I read the inscription my mother had written on the book's flyleaf: one sentence plus a fragment or two that would instantly and forever alter the way I felt about Sylvia Plath, her work, and all three of our lives:

For my wonderful daughter. Beautiful, joyous, full of
life and talent—and so much more fortunate
than Sylvia Plath. My love always darling, Mom.

All spring, as I had read and thought about Plath, I had been building an idea of her, a kind of amalgamation of facts and settings and ideas, but even as my grasp on the details of her life grew tighter, the wholeness of her—her *gestalt* (a word I had somehow managed to learn in that selfsame Freud seminar)—had seemed to be slipping away.

And that "away" was a very different place than where I was living. It was a place of chaperones and irredeemable bad girls and the rank terror of getting pregnant before marriage. Plath had had to live in a world in which being female and anything else—apart from a mother and homemaker—was as absurd as it was suspect, where a generous neighbor might offer a writer/husband with a new baby the use of a study in which to work, but never think to offer the same study to his writer/wife.

Plath's lifetime was an increasingly foreign land, the crushed-in-amber *before* of my own twentieth century—*before* civil rights, women's rights, gay rights, Wendy Wasserstein's *Uncommon Women and Others,* Paul Mazursky's *An Unmarried Woman,* or Judy Chicago's *The Dinner Party.*

Her past, and my mother's as well, was another country, and the instant I read my mother's inscription on the flyleaf of the *Journals,* I understood that. For the very first time—the first of many, many times—I felt terrible pity for Sylvia Plath.

I had been in thrall to her for the power of her work, of course, for the force of her suffering and her tragedy, but I had not begun to comprehend the crushing paradox of being a smart, ambitious woman in the 1950s and early 1960s. All those social movements separating our two generations — and the women's movement in particular — had opened up the world for me in a way she never experienced. I inherited endless possibilities, and an expectation of equality with my male classmates, the male writers I came to know, and the one I married. She got the shortened horizon shared by all pre–Second Wave women, and the overhanging fear held by the gifted among them: of being thwarted by an environment hostile to women writers, or buried by the marriage and motherhood she also desperately wanted, or made invisible in any of the countless other ways women of her time were made invisible. The great burden she lived and worked beneath was something I had never felt, not for one instant. It must have been unbearable.

I HAD MET Plath at a dangerous moment, when I might well have read the lessons of her life as a siren song of sadness and madness. But understanding that I was not obligated to suffer as Plath had suffered made it possible for me to admire, learn from, and move beyond the sorrow of her life. I would have gotten there eventually, I suppose, but without my mother's simple inscription it would have been so much harder and taken so much longer.

Nancy Milford's *New York Times* review of the *Journals* in 1982 ended with an image so powerful I have remembered it ever since: "She would be 50 this October. Instead she is forever caught in her 30th year, the fever heroine."

In 2011, I turned fifty. Unlike Plath, whose work I still revere, whose life I still respect and whose death I still mourn, I have been able to live, write, and most important of all, watch my children grow up. My mother was right: I have been so much more fortunate than Sylvia Plath.

The Unicorn Princess

KATHA POLLITT

A therapist once told me, "You never really had your mother," but she was wrong. My mother may have been an alcoholic — well, no *maybe* about it; she died of cirrhosis at only fifty-four, when I was twenty-nine. She didn't teach me the things mothers back then were supposed to, like cooking (how could she when she could hardly bake a potato herself?) or cleaning or how to behave on a date. I don't remember her helping me with my homework or reading to me at bedtime. But she loved me, she was proud of me, she wanted me to be happy, and she wanted me to be myself. Since then, from decade to decade, apartment to apartment, drawer to drawer, I've saved one gift she gave me to remind myself of that.

My mother was a beautiful woman and loved beautiful

clothes. She had a whole bureau dedicated to her collection of cashmere sweaters in deep, soft colors—butter yellow, forest green, periwinkle—and her two closets were full of treasures: Viyella dressing gowns (what other mother had more than one bathrobe?), Lilly Pulitzer sack dresses, straight skirts made of good wool, fully lined, and bearing labels from elegant department stores that no longer exist—Martin's, Peck and Peck, Bonwit Teller. My father loved to see my mother dressed up, but the money she spent on clothes drove him wild with rage. I used to hear him shouting in their bedroom when my mother's college friend Hope, who was a buyer at Altman's, would send over outfits "on approval."

I wasn't sure which side of their money quarrel I was on. I idolized my father, the communist lawyer with his parade of impecunious clients—the Fair Play for Cuba Committee, the dissidents from the painters' union, the mentally ill woman trying to get her son back from the social workers. But my mother worked, too, even in the 1950s. What's more, by the time I was nine or ten, she earned more than my father, selling brownstones in Brooklyn Heights, where we lived, which was just beginning its gentrification. She didn't like it much—she had wanted to be a journalist, a field virtually closed to women back then. But she was proud of herself for doing well. "I'm a real estate salesman," she would say—not a saleswoman, a sales*man*. Still, nobody said she was noble or heroic, which was the family myth about my father—or maybe just the myth my mother and I believed in.

In a way, my parents were a secular version of an old-style Jewish marriage. Instead of a wife peddling goods from a pushcart to support her husband, the Talmudic scholar, my mother, the capitalist, supported my father, the communist, though the rewards of being the breadwinner didn't apply to her. She still had to run the house, do the shopping, cook the food. Obviously, my father was the important one, in her eyes and also in mine. He was the person who thought about big things, like civil liberties and Stalin, and who looked so elegant in his seersucker suit. Still, I wondered as I got older, shouldn't my mother be allowed to have some fun with the money that was so hard for her to earn?

Because of these conflicts, I had trouble with the idea of spending money on myself when I was a teenager. I knew that if I asked for something, my mother would give it to me. But what if my parents couldn't afford it, like the clothes from Hope? And shouldn't I be less materialistic, anyway, like my father? After all, did communists get their bedrooms redecorated with a canopied bed, an antique secretary desk, and unicorn-printed wallpaper, which was something my mother had arranged for me with a decorator friend of hers, despite the inevitable fights with my father? "I want. Her. To have. That desk," I can still hear her insisting, emphasizing every word. And I have it to this day, in my study, catty-corner to my real desk. Poor fragile, lovely thing, how can I ever give it away?

When my bedroom was finished, it was all too much. It felt obscurely shameful, a mark of privilege, of being spoiled and overprotected, too much like the princess in whose lap the unicorn rested its head. The truth was I loved girly things — my Villager shirtwaist printed with tiny flowers, my cousin Wendy's lavender bedroom (more tiny flowers), even the unicorn wallpaper — but I could see that they led in the wrong direction. Rosa Luxemburg was just a name to me, but whatever she had done to become a world-historical person, I knew she hadn't done it wearing dresses with little flowers.

By the time I was in high school, my mother had retreated into drinking, my father was keeping her company there, and I was a raging adolescent. My idea of fashion was to wear the same turtleneck for a week. So I don't know how my mother and I came to be shopping together, and in Manhattan, too, at Fred Leighton's high-end ethnic clothing store. She saw me hesitating over a very expensive lace Mexican blouse, picking it up, putting it down, walking away, coming back. It cost what seemed like the earth to me — maybe fifty dollars.

"Do you like it, darling?" my mother asked.

"It's gorgeous," I said. It was a costume for the wallpaper unicorn princess, with alternating panels of cloth and lace, a scoop neck with lace standing up all around it, puffy elbow-length sleeves, and tiny mother-of-pearl buttons all down the back. "But it's so expensive."

"You should always get the things you really want," she said, and she picked it up, marched to the cash register, and bought it.

THE ODD THING is that I wore the blouse only once or twice. It was too fancy for high school and much too virginal for college, and anyway, like so many things we fall in love with in the store, it didn't fit right. In the mysterious way of clothes, even without my wearing it, even as it sat in one drawer after another, it somehow acquired holes and stains. To me it represents my mother's uncalized life. Selling real estate had never been the plan: she was too unworldly and gentle for all that undercutting and competition and stress. She told me once that she had started drinking in order to deal with the anxiety of meeting with clients. Sometimes I think she would have been happy just sitting in the big yellow chair in the living room and listening to Bach, drinking coffee and clipping articles from the *New York Times,* going on the occasional peace demonstration, meeting her friends or my father for lunch on Montague Street. In a way she, not I, was the real unicorn princess, only instead of being sheltered from the world in a canopy bed, she had to do battle with it every day.

But the blouse represents something happier, too, and that

is my mother's love. She wanted to do wonderful things for me, and sometimes she did—not over-the-top projects like the unicorn bedroom, but real things that helped me become myself. She never told me that I had to get married or have children, or gave me little life lessons about how to play dumb and lose gracefully to please boys. Instead, she read my poems, and when I fell in love with Latin in eighth grade and decided I wanted to learn ancient Greek, too, she found a classics major at Brooklyn College to come tutor me. She wanted to be close to me, but the drinking got in the way, and most of the time, I wouldn't let her be close, because I didn't want to end up like her. Not always, though. When I was thirteen, we went to Manhattan to see *The Lovers of Teruel,* a surrealist French dance film at the Paris Theatre, and ended up staying for three showings, we loved it so much—or was it only I who loved it so much, and she stayed for me? Sometimes on school holidays, I would meet her for hot turkey sandwiches at Sakele's, and something about our just being out of the house together, like a regular mother and daughter, would make my heart almost stop with happiness at the freedom and intimacy and fun of it. Sometimes I would come home after a sleepover at a friend's house where there had been some family tsuris, and I would feel such a sense of peace just to sit with her and my father in the garden, having a cookout like normal people, talking about normal things like school, or what a bastard President Johnson was. I'm trying to say: there were moments that shone through.

IF I DIDN'T keep that blouse, how would I remember them?

White Christmas

ANN HOOD

When I was nineteen, a junior in college, my mother gave me a very expensive, very ugly, all-white outfit for Christmas. Pants. Jacket. Shirt. Lots of white on white patterns. Hideous. This was 1976, and Izod shirts in sherbet colors were all the rage. Pink and lime and lemon yellow, with that tiny alligator grinning out at the world. Beneath them we wore brightly striped turtlenecks without folding the necks down. Over them, a different sherbet-colored sweater. In my Dorothy Hamil haircut, I walked around in a blur of color. And into this, my mother brought white, an outfit that was slightly disco when preppy had taken over.

Even worse than the trend faux pas was the way the outfit matched. With my dizzying array of colors, I worked hard to

not match. In the morning I grabbed a turtleneck, which-
ever Izod shirt was clean, and threw a sweater over it all.
Green, blue, pink, white, yellow, all thrown together. This
haphazard dressing and combinations of colors suited me.
Or rather, the girl I longed to be, the one who would lead an
unconventional, mismatched life.

But my mother, she loved for everything to match.

I had been the only second grader who had matching
shoes and purses for everything I wore. My mother would
spend hours at the mall finding the exact shade of green
accessories to compliment the stripe in a sweater, the socks
that would reveal the identical color of my blouse when they
peeked out from beneath a hem. And she didn't stop at outfits, my mother matched everything.

On many Saturday mornings, I would wake up to the
sounds of boxes being dragged up from the basement, lad-
ders squeaking open, and my mother ordering my father to
put something higher or lower. Downstairs, bedlam.

"It's Saint Patrick's Day next week," my mother would say.

Or Easter or autumn or Flag Day. And with each of these,
our entire house was converted into a theme park. Pots of
shamrocks everywhere. Green curtains hung, a green and
white tablecloth on the table. Porcelain leprechauns peered
out from behind vases and lamps. No room was safe. The
bathroom shower curtain had a shamrock pattern, the hand
towels revealed rainbows with tiny pots of gold at the end.

Green soap. Green candles. Silverware with green handles. Shamrock-printed paper napkins beside our green dishes. My parents even sipped their coffee out of green mugs.

The next week, everything turned yellow. Instead of leprechauns, baby animals stared out at me. Daffodils sat where the shamrocks had been. Our breakfast table was ablaze with yellow. "Spring!" my mother announced over her lemon-colored coffee cup.

Then it was on to Easter and then Memorial Day and then end of school, summer, Fourth of July, an endless parade of occasions to match everything around us anew.

I spent the summer I was fourteen stringing beads to make a curtain for my bedroom doorway. My father even indulged me by removing the actual door to let my creation hang there. That curtain kept the order outside my room from penetrating. The ever-revolving cast of throw rugs and pillows and curtains stayed out there. Behind my wall of beads, I taped political cartoons to the walls, burned cones of incense, and played Crosby, Stills and Nash albums loud. My mother wouldn't let me use the Indian bedspread I had bought at a small shop in downtown Providence, insisting that I keep my matching sheets and comforter. All that gingham and the white, gold-trimmed matching French provincial furniture did not keep me from plugging in a lava lamp or painting the white lamp shades in imitation Peter Max. I was a rebel, wasn't I?

In my interior life, I was a folk singer, a poet, a war protestor.

There, I lived a messy life with lots of boyfriends whom I walked barefoot with along rocky beaches. I filled notebooks with these fantasies, writing them as haiku and sonnets and tragic short stories.

"What are you doing up there?" my mother would call to me.

I couldn't answer her. There were no words to describe this yearning that itched at me, this aching to be disorderly and mismatched.

"Nothing," I'd grumble.

"Then come downstairs."

I'd close my notebook and cap my purple pen. Sighing, I'd part that curtain of beads, and enter my mother's world.

IN MY FAMILY we opened our Christmas presents on Christmas Eve after we ate a three-hour-long Italian Feast of the Seven Fishes dinner. Stuffed with calamari, *baccalà,* snails, eel, lobster, anchovies, and shrimp, we all squeezed into our tiny living room. Every year, my father had to re- move furniture to fit a giant Christmas tree, which we deco- rated with animated ornaments: trains chugged through its branches; birds popped out of silver eggs and chirped; the entire cast of a tinny "Twelve Days of Christmas" hid in bulbs and emerged out of synch, the lords a leaping and the maids a milking while the song played on and on.

Every year I made a careful list of books and records that

I wanted, gifts that my mother considered futile indulgences. Yet she did fulfill my wish list, and with each box wrapped in shiny foil that was handed to me on Christmas Eve, I hoped it was my full set of John Steinbeck books, or the Lovin' Spoonful double album. I would also get a bottle of Chanel No. 5 that lasted the whole year, and a cashmere sweater. I knew, too, that there would be clothes—outfits—that my mother had picked out, that reflected her taste, that would match right down to the buttons. Over the years, I had perfected the sigh of delight I gave when I opened these boxes. How could I tell my mother that I found these outfits dreadful? It was easier to thank her, fold them up, and tuck them away somewhere, unworn.

But this Christmas, when I opened the box and pulled the piles of white from the tissue, the desire to please and the desire to be my true self collided mightily. I pulled first the jacket—stiff, heavy white cotton-polyester blend, with a busy white pattern and large white buttons down the front—and then the pants—as stiff and heavy and white, with the same pattern—from the large white box. I stared. The outfit stared back.

"It's fitted, you know. It will show off your figure," my mother announced. "The girl said it's very popular."

I tried to duplicate my well-rehearsed sigh of delight, but instead a strangled sound came from me.

"You could wear it dancing," my mother added.

Dancing for me was done in fraternity-house basements

where boys swung me around to "Rosalita" or pressed me close while Boz Scaggs sang "Harbor Lights."

I chewed my lip, the white suit heavy on my lap. The time had come, I realized.

That white suit, the awfulness of it, gave me the courage to announce myself: a young woman who wanted to experience a world in which anything could happen, where pandemonium took preference over order. But I didn't want to hurt my mother's feelings. This was the woman who, when Peter Hayhurst broke my heart, drove me past his house just so I could gaze at it and maybe catch a glimpse of him. When I was nine, she told me I could marry Paul McCartney if I set my mind to it. She encouraged my love of reading, and read the stories I wrote. In fact, I took all of my carefully coordinated outfits to college with me just so she wouldn't feel bad. That was why I had boxes of scarves and socks in every color imaginable in my closet, beside the boxes of holiday theme items she sent me: the orange towels and ceramic pumpkins, the cornucopia and the pilgrim statues.

But that Christmas, I took a deep breath and announced myself. I was not someone who would wear this white suit, I said. I did not want to match, I said.

My mother, dressed in Christmas red from head to toe, smiled.

"Not your thing?" she asked.

I shook my head, studying her for signs of betrayal or disappointment or hurt. But found none.

"Bring it back," she said easily.

She went to the drawer where neat files held receipts and cancelled checks, pens, paper clips, stamps. Everything in its place. She handed me the receipt for the white outfit.

"Now, *I* would wear this if I was younger," she said, folding it perfectly back into the box.

I could never fit things into the box from which they had come. I could never get a map back into a rectangle or match the corners of a fitted sheet.

Behind us, the train circling the tree's branches blew its horn and the endless rendition of "The Twelve Days of Christmas" played. The lights blinked on and off, sending blues and green, red and pink into the room.

"But then, you're not me," she said.

The way she said it, I understood that she had known this all along.

A mother's love is like that. I know this now that I'm a mother. We give our children the best of ourselves so that they can find the best of what is in them. The day I rejected the gift of the white suit, I got the best gift of all. My mother let me know that I had finally become that person I'd dreamed of becoming: a girl who spoke her mind, who was independent and opinionated. A girl who knew who she was and what she wanted. A girl who would not wear an all-white pants suit. And by recognizing that, she gave me permission to go into my own mismatched future. What a gift.

My Mother's Armor

MARGO JEFFERSON

"Look back, Mama. What were your favorite clothes?" I asked
her this year. She's ninety-five, and we had come back from a
luncheon with her birthday club. She had worn wine-colored
wool pants, a gray sweater with a touch of sparkle, pearls, and
a black cape. She'd finally decided on wine instead of gray — "I
don't want monotony" — and I'd fussed a bit because our ride
was waiting while she chose her handkerchief. "Are you ready?"
I asked, when she'd slipped a white lace-trimmed one into her
purse. "Have you put on cologne?" she answered. I had not and
so I did. Then we were both ready.

And now we were home again, lounging in the living room.
"What were your favorite clothes?" I asked.

"My evening dresses," was her answer. This surprised me a bit. She'd loved hats: I'd anticipated total recall of millinery triumphs in sisal or felt. (I'd been in awe of a cream-colored Tastee Freez swirl of a hat with a black veil.)

"Short or long evening dresses?"

"Both."

"What was the difference?"

"The short ones were flip and flirty."

"And the long ones?"

She laughed and put one hand to her forehead, fingers arranged in a classic heroine-about-to-swoon pose. "Beware my foolish heart," she drawled.

The night is like a lovely tune,
Beware my foolish heart . . .

That ballad appeared in 1949, when my mother was thirty-three and I was three; I like to imagine my parents moving onto the dance floor as the orchestra took a sumptuous lyric plunge into its opening notes.

"My Foolish Heart," "Lush Life," "Stardust," "Misty," "Sophisticated Lady." I heard these songs over and over on our record player. The flip and flirty numbers, too, deft syncopations of wit, lust, and romance. "That Old Black Magic," "Do Nothing Till You Hear from Me," "Gee Baby, Ain't I Good to You?" And of course that urbane salty blues which hailed our city:

Goin' to Chicago,
Sorry but I can't take you.

Those proud Chicago department stores we shopped in! Marshall Field and Chas. A. Stevens, designed by the firm of D. H. Burnham, the architect who'd ruled the World's Fair. Carson, Pirie, Scott, designed by Louis B. Sullivan, master builder of the skyscraper. Mighty structures of granite and terra-cotta; arrogantly eclectic with their escalators and Tiffany lamps, their modernist lines and Renaissance flourishes. They sat in the city's commercial center, the downtown Loop, flanked by hotels, theaters, and office buildings. Proclaiming the union of exclusivity and accessibility.

Today's common wisdom says we're inundated with sensory data, bombarded by images. But it started long ago — these late nineteenth- and early twentieth-century department stores were the first to make sensory bombardment a stately art. They were the self-contained ancestors of the mall. Counter after counter of lipsticks, powders, perfumes; cases filled with gloves (wrist-length, mid-arm, lined, unlined, cotton, suede kid, white, cream, black, tan); leather goods; candies — and we haven't even reached the escalators. We're still on the ground floor, which stretches across two city blocks.

For girls like my sister and me, bourgeois girls of the 1950s and early '60s, shopping was an intricately plotted expedition. Our mother was the leader and guide. She showed us what to look for as our eyes wandered and wondered. She showed us what to pass by. *She* directed the gaze.

Marshall Field, where Mother took us to sit on Santa's knee at Christmas in a maze of giant wreaths, candy canes, and glazed whirling ornaments.

Marshall Field, where Mother took us to lunch at the Walnut Room.

Marshall Field's 28 Shop, where Mother told her mother, "You really shouldn't smoke here," and her mother answered, "As much as I pay for these clothes, I'll do what I want."

Marshall Field, where my father's aunt Nancy passed for white to work as a saleswoman in the 1920s.

AT SAKS AND Bonwit Teller the exclusivity-accessibility balance shifted. They were smaller, more discreet stores. They were on the posh Near North Side, not in the "come hither all ye consumers" Loop. The rhythm of buying and selling was more decorous, the conversation quieter. And you knew when you entered that fewer people felt they could take the liberty—claim the right—to simply walk through as tourists. Mother didn't take us there before 1960. As Negroes we had to secure our place downtown before we ventured North.

EVERY MONTH A coffee-table-sized *Vogue* arrived at our house. Every month I devoured it. The models were

starting to be known by name. My favorite was red-haired
Suzy Parker: tall and lissome, her face a perfect assemblage of
curves (the lips, the eyebrows) and lines (the nose, the cheekbones). The models wore the grand European designs of Dior,
Givenchy, Balenciaga, and Madame Grès. They showed off the
clothes of Americans with rhythmically deft, alliterative names:
Norman Norell, Bill Blass, Geoffrey Beene. They were muses
and fetish objects, sumptuous offerings on the altar of feminine
glamour.

And I worshipped offerings to feminine glamour, in magazines, movies, and in life. The clothes; the lingerie; the array of
handkerchiefs, some lace-trimmed, some initialed; pocketbooks
of leather and alligator, bearing their own mirrors and coin
purses; peau-de-soie clutch bags for evening or small beaded
ones with handles that just slipped over your wrist. The perfume and cologne bottles on Mother's vanity table and dresser.
The earrings, bracelets, necklaces arranged in the leather jewelry box with its Florentine design.

I learned to accept the verbotens, too. One summer day I
came downstairs wearing a red blouse and a purple and white
flowered skirt; I was sent right back upstairs to change. You
don't wear certain colors together, especially loud colors.
Denim is only for weekend play and summer camp. Little girls
don't wear nail polish. Little girls wear *white* socks with their
Mary Janes.

I accepted the verbotens because I longed to be a perfect girl, and if a girl lacked perfect prettiness—which I did—then this was a route to compensatory perfection. I accepted the verbotens because they came from my mother, whose appearance and manner I found both authoritative and deeply pleasing: her crisp Claudette Colbert hairdo; her five-foot-three-inch frame, trim and shapely, but not skinny; her smooth beige-brown skin. She was witty, lively, and chic. So were her friends. I loved how they looked in their suits and silk shirtwaists, their furs and smart hats. I loved how they carried themselves at luncheons and parties, or when they took us to plays or concerts. I loved the quick comments and judgments they flung out. They were in full command.

And yet, they were almost entirely absent from the main stage of feminine glamour, from *Vogue,* from *Harper's Bazaar,* from *Life* and *Look,* from television, from movies. Race had decreed it so.

How did I register the fact that everyone who mattered in this vast beauty-and-fashion complex was white? Not until the 1960s did models of color start making their presence felt. Headline, 1962: Photographer Gordon Parks—a Negro himself!—photographs a *Life* spread on "exotic" clothes titled, "Swirl of Bright Hues: New Styles Shown by Negro Models—A Band of Beautiful Pioneers." Headline, 1966: Donyale Luna becomes the first Negro model to make the cover of *Vogue.*

Feminism has taught us how the beauty-and-fashion

complex maims girls and women. It invents styles and standards that create impossible longings. If you're smitten, your cravings start early. You want something—some feature, some body part, some look or aura—you do not have and will not ever have.

Those cheekbones, which make the thought of a skull erotic;
Those rosebud lips, so sweetly small;
Those tapering fingers which gloves clung to;
That sleek neck, that long torso, those lean kinetic-sculpture legs;
The delicate whimsy of Audrey Hepburn;
The sultry lushness of Elizabeth Taylor;
The country-club sangfroid of Grace Kelly.

Begin with those biological impossibilities. Then add the racial one: No! you cannot ever be white like these idols of feminine perfection. Let that final impossibility reproach and taunt you.

Nevertheless, a separate world of colored/Negro/black/African-American beauty and glamour did exist. Every month a coffee-table-sized *Ebony* arrived at our house. Every month I studied its cream, beige, tan, buff, brown, and sepia models. Every month I read its tales of people like us, who achieved against all odds and carried the race forward.

My favorite model was Dorothea Towles. She was just six years younger than Mother. Mother even knew her. She'd gone to college (as we were expected to do); she'd married a dentist (we were expected to marry professionals); she'd decided to follow her sister to Paris (a concert pianist, which we admired). And there she'd broken ranks to fulfill our wild secret fantasies of Josephine Baker crossed with Audrey Hepburn in *Funny Face:* she'd gone to the house of Dior, become a model, and gone from there to Schiaparelli and Balmain.

I admired her, I envied her, but I didn't worship her as I worshipped Suzy Parker. She was in *Ebony* not *Vogue.* That meant she was not being universally looked up to. She was not being noticed.

When I look at pictures of her now, I realize just how adorable Dorothea was. She had the kinetic-sculpture legs, the tapering fingers, a sleek neck and shoulders. I say "adorable" because her face was piquant. The high cheekbones were there, but their shape was softly round (like Baker's). The full lower lip was there, the pouty lip that would be so desirable in the '60s and '70s. Her dark eyes had a playful, almost quizzical expression, as if she were amused to watch the world watch her. Her hair was dark, too—except when she chose to dye it blond.

Did she turn her back on her people? Certainly not! Did she return to bourgeois obscurity as a dentist's wife? Not that either. She did return to the United States in 1954, and she did leave her husband for good. Then using her own numerous haute-couture clothes, she barnstormed the country, organizing all-black fashion shows for all-black sororities and charities. *Jet* loved to chronicle her flamboyant doings, enhanced by flamboyant photos: "Model Dorothea Towles created a sensation when she strolled into a white fur shop in Birmingham and asked to rent $10,000 worth of furs for the AKA's fashion show. The owner sent along three private cops to guard the furs." This alongside a picture of pert, carefree Towles at the beach, perched on a rock in a two-piece strapless bathing suit, high-heeled ankle-strap sandals, and a wide, fringed straw hat.

Please note that Dorothea Towles returned to America the year the Supreme Court decreed segregation illegal in public schools. Separate but equal was being challenged on all fronts. And four years later, my mother's friend Eunice Johnson took up that challenge, expanding what Dorothea Towles had begun. Her husband, John H. Johnson, published *Ebony, Jet, Sepia,* and *Negro Digest.* She gave *Ebony* its bold, pre–Black Power name. She became the company's secretary-treasurer and aesthetic advisor. Now she launched the Ebony Fashion Fair, a touring fashion show on a grander scale. She didn't use her own clothes, as Towles had. She'd go to the top shows in Paris and Milan, sit in front-row seats beside white editors and buy clothes. She'd go to the top shows in New York, sit in front-row seats beside white editors and buy clothes. She'd go in search of young black designers and buy clothes. Beige, tan, buff, cream, sepia, brown, and (eventually) ebony models strode and sashayed down hotel runways in city after city, wearing these clothes for colored/Negro/black and African-American audiences. It was spectacular.

We were still separate, but under Eunice's direction we were equal and sufficient unto the day. No, we were not wholly equal—the white world was still dominant. It had made the rules that excluded us; when it saw fit, it altered those rules to include *some* of us. Politics was changing the culture; the aesthetics of fashion and glamour were changing, too. But we had been there all along. Before they noticed or acknowledged us, we were there.

I OFTEN LOOK through the clothes my mother has seen fit to give me through the years. (I never cease to regret the ones she gave away.) I cherish the Pauline Trigère brushed wool, funnel-shaped coat, beige with thin stripes of pale mauve, lilac, blue, and white. Such quiet symmetry it could be wallpaper. I feel like a craft object when I close my body into this coat. And I feel vindicated, too, because Pauline Trigère was the first top American designer to use a black model regularly. We always knew these things; *Jet,* *Ebony,* or our mothers told us.

Brava Madame Trigère! Still, the piece I most love wearing is Mother's gold brocade cocktail dress with matching jacket. It was designed by Malcolm Starr, best known for bejeweled '60s evening wear. The dress is sleeveless, with wide straps, a nipped waist, and a wraparound-style skirt. Not a wide skirt, but wide enough for a feminist to walk in without mincing her steps. The waist-length jacket is trimmed in gold braid; so is the skirt's front panel.

It's "flip and flirty" as my mother prescribed. It's crisp yet splendid. It makes me feel I've put on made-to-order armor.

My mother's armor.

Armor that helped shield me from exclusion.

Armor that shielded me from inferiority.

Three-Hour Tour

EMMA STRAUB

When I was in graduate school, I lived in Madison, Wisconsin, on a narrow spit of land between two lakes. The actual word for this land formation is an *isthmus,* but no one who is not a crossword puzzle champion or a resident of said city knows what that means. I lived closer to the smaller lake, Monona, which is famous for being where Otis Redding crashed his airplane and died. The larger lake, Mendota, was where all the college kids did their boat-sailing and suntanning. I paid neither lake much attention, other than taking walks nearby and sometimes stopping to watch the water move in the sun (summertime) or watch the ice stand still (wintertime).

In the warmer months, when the lakes weren't frozen, a small charter company called Betty Lou Cruises took groups of people out on the water for what can only very generously be described as "tours." I sometimes saw these groups standing together in the parking lot beside one of the docks when I went to brunch, and my first thought was always, *Oh, how sad and strange.* One could walk around the entire lake in a few hours, forty-five minutes on a bicycle. The path went by sweet-looking houses and parks in Madison, and through a suburb on the far side of the lake. The whole enterprise struck me as a thing that people did when they had already exhausted everything pleasurable, or when family visits went on too long and one simply *had* to get out of the house.

My mother, a Wisconsinite by birth and a New Yorker by choice, felt differently. A friend, a local travel agent, had told her about the cruises, and my mother thought they sounded charming. She sent me a gift certificate for my birthday, passes for two, on the lake of our choice. This did not surprise me. My mother's mother had a closet full of Ferragamo shoes, endless strings of pearls, and she never washed her own hair, and so perhaps it makes sense that her daughter went in the opposite direction for herself and for me. My mother long ago stopped buying me clothing, or jewelry, or anything remotely girly. Instead, we look at art together, or she springs for "experiential" presents, which she claims last longer in the memory. In theory, I agree, and think such presents are wonderful. In practice, I had zero desire to spend three hours on a lake the size of the Central Park reservoir.

The gift certificate sat on my desk for months while I was in graduate school, too busy writing stories and reading books to care much about the outside world. I moved to a different apartment, and the gift certificate moved with me. My mother and I speak on the telephone nearly every day, and every so often, she would ask whether I had gone on the cruise yet. Eventually, it made me feel so guilty that I looked for the damn thing, determined to use it before I left Wisconsin, which was suddenly nigh on the horizon. And it was gone.

I panicked. Surely the folks at Betty Lou kept careful records? I called. They didn't. My choices were as follows: I could either call my mother and tell her that I'd gone on the cruise, lying through my teeth, or I could do the grown-up thing. I am a horrendous liar, and so the choice was clear. I bought tickets for myself and my husband — forty dollars each — and on a rainy morning in October, we lined up on the dock and waited to board. BETTY LOU CRUISES was written in script on the side of the double-decker boat, the upper level hemmed in by a waterproof blue tarp. From close-up, I could tell how small the boat really was, not to mention the lake it was sitting in.

The boat smelled like gasoline, as boats often do. We filed on, though I was fairly sure that the boat was about to explode. I figured that if something *did* happen, I would only have to swim about ten feet back to the shore, where I could climb back up and go to brunch on land, as I would have preferred. My husband shot me a withering look, already deeply miserable himself.

Captain Steve greeted us in a yellow rain slicker and a monogrammed baseball hat that read CAPTAIN STEVE. We quickly took seats near a window, as the rain was coming down just enough so that being outside would have necessitated one of Steve's slickers. Other, braver folks — women in belted leather jackets and plastic rain bonnets — took in the view from the outer deck. As we departed, I heard the faintest strains of Otis Redding's "(Sittin' on) the Dock of the Bay" coming through the loudspeakers. No one remarked upon this, but it struck me as both ominous and vaguely threatening, as in, *This lake only looks safe.* I began to worry that three hours might be too much time. Captain Steve steered us to the right, taking the lake in a clockwise motion. He announced over the microphone, "Here's your first view of Monona Terrace," the Frank Lloyd Wright–designed conference center close to the dock. The first of many views, we all understood, because Monona Terrace was the only architectural milestone on the lake.

But the bar was open, and the warming trays were warmed, and we all helped ourselves to small plastic glasses of champagne and orange juice, or Bloody Marys, and to heaping plates of French toast covered with candied pecans. There were inch-thick slabs of pink prime rib, for those eager to move on to lunch, and hash browns smothered with cheese. Everyone piled their plates high, and went back for seconds. Most people clustered around the bar, and the one Asian family on board stuck close to Captain Steve, who pointed out things to them that the rest of us didn't see. A legless man in a wheelchair faced a window. Someone had brought a baby, who was crying, but we were by far the youngest patrons who had come of their own volition. My husband tugged his hooded sweatshirt around his face to block out the noise and the cold, misty wind off the water and, I thought, in an attempt to enter a one-person witness protection program.

We circled the lake once, and I got as excited as a puppy at the sight of the dock, but no, of course not yet. We circled the entire lake again then, then a third time. By the time we hit a rock, temporarily halting our voyage, I began to wonder if we would ever disembark, or if I had willingly signed us up for the maritime version of *No Exit*, where we would be with the rain-bonneted ladies and Captain Steve for the rest of our lives. Relaxing into the pain, my husband and I took photos of each other, and the rainy deck of the boat, and our food. The lake itself looked gray and uninviting, but I thought I could still swim back to shore if necessary. The water would be cold, but I would get home faster.

After our misbegotten shipwreck, Captain Steve revved the engine enough to knock the rock loose, and we were again on our way. By the time the boat had again reached the dock, my husband and I were feeling solid on our sea legs, and rushed toward the plank that would bring us back to land. As soon as we rounded the corner onto the leafy residential street that would bring us home, I called my mother to tell her that we had finally taken the cruise, and then described it to her, second by second, while she laughed, her hooting and snorting keeping me warm as we walked the four blocks home.

I don't remember many of the gifts that my mother has given me—though a knockoff watchband from Chinatown and bags of Margarita Mix from her pantry do come to mind. But when I think of her, I don't think of objects. I think of walking somewhere with her, arm in arm, our laughs always the loudest in any room, or her clapping along with whatever music is playing, always having more fun than anyone else. If my mother had come on the boat with us, she would have hummed along with Otis Redding and introduced herself to Captain Steve. She would have been driving the boat, rain bonnet or no, happy as could be. My own happiness during every terrible minute of the Betty Lou Cruise came from knowing that when it ended, I would get to tell her all about it.

The Circle Line

．．．

MARY GORDON

She throws an envelope onto the kitchen table, vaguely in my direction. She has written my name on it, and underlined it twice. I know what's in it: it's my birthday and inside the envelope there will be, as always, a check. I am only ten years old, and I do not exactly know what to do with money, and I wish my mother had bought me a present, like other people's mothers. But the only time I expressed that wish she answered, sharply, harshly, "Who the hell could figure out what you want?" So I'm not getting a present like other kids, and it is—somehow—my fault.

This is the scene that came into my mind when I was asked about a favorite gift from my mother. My first response was, "My mother never gave me any gifts." These words were followed by a generous helping of self-pity: that sickish sweet, oily syrup that somehow encourages the tongue and the palate to demand more and more. I try to stay away from its allure, and so, when I feel it coming on (particularly when its source is my mother), I seek alternatives. I begin by going the route of Marx or Freud: my mother was working class, the child of immigrants, her young womanhood lived out against the backdrop of the Depression. Or: her childhood was difficult; she was the oldest of nine children of a harsh mother; she was stricken with polio at the age of three, an affliction which made it impossible that she would love her body. She was a single working mother, a widow, living with her grief-stricken child, her demanding mother, her jealous sister: she of the gimlet eye and viper tongue. And so, finally, I push both Marx and Freud into the background and settle on a simpler explanation: She was worn out. She was tired.

One of my mother's most treasured ways of identifying herself was to let everyone know that she wasn't like other women. She spoke of everything connected to the traditionally feminine with a lacerating contempt. The decoration of houses, the preparation of food (even the discussion of food), hair, makeup, clothing—all these were the property of a category she referred to as "lightweights." I have come to understand that this was a complicated defense against what life didn't give her, what she couldn't have. Her polio meant that her body would never be acceptable by conventional standards. It was probably easier for her not to look at it too closely; buying clothes would have required this kind of self-scrutiny, a scrutiny that was, for her, a very bad bet indeed. Better to say she was above all that, beyond all that. To relegate that to the "lightweights." As she relegated cooking and interior decoration because she never had the kind of marriage (my father earned no money; his contribution to our financial life was to get us into debt) that would allow the kind of leisure that attention to cooking and decoration might require. So she relegated the domestic realm to lightweights as well.

What was the opposite of a lightweight? It wasn't a heavyweight. It did not mean a person who was earnest or even serious. These people were rejected out of hand as "sad sacks" or "pains in the ass." Humor was the coin of the realm. Its products were her treasured capital. Jokes were important, jokes were essential; a satiric commentary on the follies of one's fellow humans was a pearl of great price. Some things, though, were of critical importance. Anything having to do with the success and superiority of the Roman Catholic Church was always welcome. Anything pointing out the inferiority of the Republican Party was just fine. But jokes, religion, and politics—where could you buy them? How could you wrap them? What color would be preferable? Did you want them large or small? All the things my mother prized, being incorporeal, did not make themselves available as gifts.

You may wonder why my mother didn't buy me books. The

answer was simple: she didn't trust her taste. My father was the reader and writer in the family, and she realized when I was very young (my father taught me to read at three) that books were his province, his and mine. We were the superior inhabitants of a superior realm, a territory she wouldn't have dreamed of trespassing upon. When he died, when I was seven, she left the selection of my reading material to two of her closest friends, both of whom had been to college. She had only finished high school, and though she knew herself to be intelligent, she was fastidious at granting intellectual pride of place to those with what she considered superior credentials.

And so, I have come to understand why she never got me presents, and this failure was the objective correlative of her inability to give me any useful guidance on a good way of being a woman. This, too, has been a cause for generous lashings of self-pity when I drink the hemlock of deprivation and regret for what I have not had, or what I had to earn or win myself, through luck or labor.

I THOUGHT NO more about the question of my mother and her gifts, or lack of them. And one day — it was a sparkling late afternoon in the middle of May — I was in a cab driving down the West Side Highway. The sun glimmered on the river; coin-sized patches of light danced along the Hudson's silver skin. My eye fell on a rather

unprepossessing boat; I heard its cheerful, workmanlike toot-
ing. I saw the sign spelled out in white along its sides. CIRCLE
LINE, it said.

Immediately, I am back more than fifty years. It is a spring
day, but an earlier one: the beginning of April. Easter vacation.
My mother has taken a day off. "We're going on a little adventure," she tells me. She has booked tickets for Circle Line: the
boat that takes people around Manhattan Island.

I remember, driving next to her in our two-toned blue Nash
Rambler, a high sense of rightness, but a rightness whose exalta-
tion nevertheless felt entirely secure and safe. My mother was
driving me on "an adventure." She had taken a day off. We were
going to the city. Not only to the city: we were going on a boat.
No one we knew had ever done this. It was something people
talked about doing, but never did. And we were doing it!

I don't remember how long the voyage took. I remember sitting next to her and eating ham sandwiches we'd brought from
home. I remember bringing her a coffee from the bar inside
the boat; I selected, for myself, a lemonade. The air smelled
wonderfully of salt and the larger world. "There's the Statue
of Liberty," my mother said. We picked out the Empire State
Building. Neither of which we'd ever actually visited, or, being
New Yorkers, were likely to do. I was so proud of her, and of
myself as her daughter. She had taken a day off! She had had
this wonderful idea! She had made everything possible. Everything that no one else could have done.

It occurred to me that day, fifty years later on the West Side Highway, that this was a very great gift indeed. Better than a Ginny doll or an angora sweater or a poodle skirt or a heart-shaped locket or a gold bracelet or my first pair of high heels. She was giving me the gift of the larger world. And the belief that it was something that could be reached. If you just thought of it, and figured out how to make it happen. This was the reward for not being like other women. This was our reward for not being like other mothers and daughters. An adventure on the water. The sight of the glittering city. The possibility of the greater world.

The Gift Twice Given

. . . .

JUDITH HILLMAN PATERSON

"Your mother is dead. Forget about it." Said or unsaid, the message was clear. Forget her and your life as it used to be.

My fourth-grade teacher told the others my mother had died that summer. They were to be nice to me but not mention it. I remember nothing about either the first day of school that year or my birthday. No presents. No cake. I remember loneliness, confusion, and my father's devastating grief. My life depended on him—a dead man walking.

He soon married my stepmother, Dot, the war widow of a distant cousin. I loved my father, a depressive alcoholic with a scary temper, and was as bonded to him as if I had come out of his body instead of my mother's. Dot wanted to fix what ailed us. I missed my mother and withdrew into books and the rolling landscape around the house my parents had built in the country outside Montgomery, Alabama.

I was the oldest child of four. Five, if you count the brother who died after three days when I was four, leaving an ever-festering wound at the heart of our family. My sister Jane had been born a year and two days after me. Momma was already sick even then. Jane did not like school or rolling hills. She was a witty, reckless girl who'd say anything to get attention. Out of the blue, she'd call out "Momma" or "our brother who died" like some oracle child fetching lost souls from the deep.

She'd get louder and louder until Daddy exploded and left the house and Dot unloaded a tirade of vitriol on my triumphant sister. I froze every time and either said nothing or growled between my teeth: "Damn it, Jane. Shut up. Now look, he's gone. He'll drink. He'll kill himself in the car. Dot will be scared till he gets back, and then she'll be mad."

How are children to grieve in such a household? One parent in the grave and the other half-crazed with guilt and sorrow and four children to raise.

By the time Momma died, I'd been expecting it for years. She didn't eat. She had migraines. She couldn't sleep at night. She took sleeping pills, pain pills, Stanback, paregoric. She drank beer and slept in the daytime—or cried in her room. When she was hospitalized, for short and long periods of time, we stayed either with Daddy's mother, Gram, or at home with a young black woman named Mary Willie Jackson, who sang show tunes and blues and taught us to fish with a pole and catch frogs with our hands. She told us about cities far away where she planned to go someday.

Mary Willie was still in high school when she started staying with us. Gram thought she had "big ideas" and never did "a lick of work around the house," but Momma was crazy about her and so were we. After a few years, she married a soldier named Leroy who was stationed at the air base. Leroy stuck his chest out and stood so straight I thought the buttons would pop off his uniform. "Uppity," Daddy said, narrowing his eyes. A threat to our household.

Mary Willie got dressed up and went off with Leroy sometimes, but she always came back. She'd never leave us, she said. Leroy was just a man and didn't we know a man is "a two-face, a worrisome thing who'll lead you to sing the bluuuues in the night"?

Momma was seriously addicted to alcohol and prescription drugs by the time our doomed brother was born and died. Daddy blamed her. She had a breakdown, left on the train, and said she wouldn't be back. You'd think that would have been the end of it, but Daddy went and got her.

A few months later, the Japanese attacked Pearl Harbor. My father wanted to fight for democracy. Momma said she'd die if he left her. My second sister, Joan, was born the following September, as puny as our dead brother had been. With undeveloped lungs and an exposed thymus gland, she came home without a name, not expected to live. She lived anyway and grew up to be an odd child with developmental delays and a spirit so generous it put us all to shame.

Daddy joined the Construction Battalion of the navy (the Seabees) and got ready to go to Lido Beach on Long Island for training. If you ask me, he had good reason to fly the coop but he was also patriotic. We were to stay in a rented house in town where Gram, Mary Willie, and Momma's Aunt Bessie could help out.

Momma lasted only a few months before she broke down again, thinking she was dying and threatening suicide unless we could join Daddy in New York. Off we went on the train with Gram, Mary Willie, and Momma, who talked the conductor into letting Mary Willie sit in the whites-only coach, saying she was needed to look after Joan. *All aboard, chickens. This ain't the Chattanooga Choo Choo. We headed for Nuuu Yaaawk!*

We got a house on Long Beach beside a canal. Daddy came home a lot at first. Jane and I went to a progressive school in a little bus with other children and played in snow for the first time. Gram helped us get settled. Then she went home. Aunt Bessie came and fought with Momma over the pills she took and read stories to Jane and me. She took us to the Bronx Zoo and to the city to buy winter coats at Best & Company. Then she went home. My uncle who was in the army and my aunt and my cousin came for a few days. Mary Willie was with us most of the time. Our first months in New York were both an extension of home and a big adventure.

Everybody knew the Allies planned to invade France. Nobody knew when or where. Daddy was too busy to leave the base. Gram and Aunt Bessie were gone. Mary Willie left for a few days with Leroy before he went overseas. Momma drank. And drank and drank. She slept so long and hard I had to check to be sure she was breathing. We stopped going to school and never went back.

Until then, I had not realized my mother was truly unable to care for us. Joan was almost two, but very small. She wasn't potty trained, couldn't walk, and still ate baby food. I had a phone number to call friends of Daddy's but I thought he'd be mad if I did. One day, Momma got up and said, "Don't light the stove," then went back to bed. Somehow we looked after Joan. I learned to pray sitting at the window waiting for Daddy to come home. Finally, he did. Mary Willie came back, but Momma kept drinking and sleeping.

Then it was spring and Momma was pregnant. A doctor said unless she stopped drinking, the baby would die like our brother or be sickly like Joan. Daddy went to France after D-day, and we went back to Montgomery, and a neighborhood filled with playmates. Though I was coming up on my eighth birthday, I had yet to attend a full year of school.

Prior to that year, I remember my mother mainly as a

temperamental, girlish invalid, too preoccupied with her own anguish to relate to her children. My first eight years are nearly empty of memories of any homemaking or mothering on her part. No bathing or dressing or cooking or feeding or playing or reading or singing or dancing.

Now, in that little house with Daddy gone, Mary Willie there, and many of my mother's friends in town for the duration of the war, my mother stayed mostly sober and functional for the better part of a year and a half. I do not know what mysterious combination of will power, family support, and the grace of God enabled her to do it.

For the first time in my life, she looked after me. She tended to things. She took me with her to the gift shop where she drank tea and rented novels. We went Christmas shopping and wrapped presents, doing the ordinary things mothers do with their children. For the first time, I experienced my mother's love as daily life rather than an abstraction.

She read to me, watched over me, gave me my first birthday party when I turned nine, paid attention to my friends, and was unduly proud of how fast I caught up in school. Though her own adolescent anxieties had caused her to drop out of three high schools before calling it quits, she loved helping me with homework. I remember her sitting at the kitchen table night after night with her legs crossed, one foot swinging, a cigarette in one hand and the script in the other, teaching me my part in a school play.

Occasionally, she and Mary Willie took us to see the monkeys at Oak Park and to throw peanuts at Polly, a parrot that had once belonged to her family. Polly knew Momma's name. If we tried hard enough we could get her to screech, "Emily . . . Emily . . . Polly want a cracker . . . Emily . . . Emily."

When her own mother died the next summer in Montgomery, Momma and I spent two days cleaning out her mother's antique-cluttered apartment. I'd heard tales of Momma's girlhood athletic prowess, but I'd never before seen her do work of any sort. Her skill and energy surprised me. We sent the furniture off in a van and took home two leather trunks filled with scrapbooks, clippings, fur coats, and flapperish dresses and shoes.

"I just have to keep these; they have Knoxie written all over them," is all she had to say about her neglectful and self-indulgent mother who preferred to be called by her given name.

I saw that beneath the childlike invalid Momma had seemed to be, there lay a lively and capable woman. I loved being alone with her and helping her do things.

Those months back in Montgomery transformed my relationship with my mother as magically as if we had been characters in a fairy tale set free of bewitchment. She gave me all she had to give—and I took it, as greedy and unthinking as a suckling pig.

My brother Jim was born healthy in January 1945. The war ended in August. Momma had already begun drinking intermittently by the time Daddy returned in November. Some say a drinking friend tempted her to it. Some say that's just what addicts do. Or was there something in the prospect of isolation in the country and the return of my father she just couldn't face?

Despite interruptions, Momma's attempts at sobriety and our closeness continued. Daddy had been told that her drinking could kill her, and that she'd never be able to stop unless he stopped with her. They tried and failed, tried and failed, and by the next August she was gone. *Your mother is dead. Forget her.*

Soon Mary Willie was gone. Forget her, too. Gone because she belonged to the past that included my mother. Willie had her own way of doing things. She talked about Momma. She let us run wild. We kissed her on the mouth. She had to go.

Gone. Nobody said she wouldn't be back. She'd always come back before. "When is Willie coming back?" "Where is Willie?" I suppose I eventually stopped asking. I don't remember.

A few months (or was it years?) later, I overheard Daddy tell Gram, "Leroy wrote from Detroit asking to borrow a hundred dollars. I sent it. Don't tell Dot." Gram gave a disapproving snort. I pretended not to hear.

And so I went on, had a growth spurt, made friends, excelled in school, and seemed to forget. At home, I got along well enough minus occasional spells of despair and outbursts of temper.

But I didn't forget Momma. I just didn't think about her. When scraps of memory floated by—which they regularly did—I'd wince and bat them away like gnats before my eyes. Remembered emotions grew shadowy, unfelt, and unattached to time. Not forgotten, not repressed, just pushed aside. Daddy rarely said my mother's name. Nobody spoke it in his presence. The word *Emily* filled me with foreboding.

After I married and had children, I'd sometimes be surprised by a phrase, a gesture, or a tone of voice that seemed to come not from me but from Momma or Willie or some combination of the two. Saying "dahlin'" or "sugah" in Momma's way or "gal" or "chickin" in Willie's. Momma's humming, "I found my thrill on Blueberry Hill" or Willie's "Man got a heart like a rock cast in the sea."

One day my nine-year-old daughter, Beth, returned from playing at the home of her friend's grandmother and said to me, "Kathy's grandmother's name is Emily. She told me to call her Emily."

"That was my mother's name."

"What?"

"That was my mother's name."

"I thought Dot was your mother."

I was stunned. How in the world had I managed to wipe

out the first decade of my life—including every trace of my
mother's existence? It was the same number of years that
Beth and I had been daughter and mother. No photographs.
No treasured objects. No favorite stories. Not a word.

Beth had no idea that her blood grandmother had ever
existed. Neither did her brother. Jane's children also didn't
know. Even my volatile sister had been silenced.

THINGS DID NOT go well for my father's children.
By 1980, all of us were divorced. I knew how to work and
ignore disappointment. I knew how to love only in part. I
did not know how to grieve. After my divorce, I moved to
Washington, D.C. It was around that time that I began to
think about my mother and the troubles in our family.

I asked Daddy to help me find Mary Willie. He said he
didn't remember Leroy's last name, hadn't heard from them
in years. The next time I was home, he said he'd driven out
the Selma Highway to where she'd lived in a colored settle-
ment now called the City of St. Jude, which had welcomed
the Selma marchers in 1965. The house was gone, the streets
looked different, nobody remembered Mary Willie. I imagined Daddy, an old white man sick with lung cancer, going
door to door in a black neighborhood. He used to know
people out there. Not anymore.

He put his elbows on his knees, his head in his hands,

heaved a sob, got up and left the room. His sorrow overwhelmed me. I dropped the subject and set about making a living in Washington.

Daddy died in 1985. My forty-one-year-old brother died a year later. With the two great loves of her life gone, Dot lasted only a year and a half. My sisters were fighting their own addictions, and it fell to me to dismantle and sell the house our parents had built.

I divided its contents among family members before driving back to Washington with a carload of memorabilia, including the two trunks Momma and I had packed at Knoxie's in the summer of 1945. I had written three books by then and enough articles to get tenured in the English Department at Auburn University in Montgomery, and be on my way to doing the same in the College of Journalism at the University of Maryland. But until that summer, I had rarely written anything in the first person. Not me. Too personal. Too scary.

But the losses of a lifetime had caught up with me. And, before school started in the fall, I had begun a series of newspaper and magazine columns that drew on my family's experience with alcoholism, mental illness, and grief. They were like nothing I had written before.

I spent the next ten years digging through family documents, interviewing lost relatives and friends, trudging from my house to the Library of Congress and the National Archives, and traveling across the Deep South, Virginia, Kentucky, Ohio, and New York, trying to understand my family and the meaning of Momma's death. It didn't take long to locate the mighty river of depression, anxiety, and addiction that ran in her family. There was something else, too, harder to define—a certain lack of meaning in their lives or faith in themselves, some way in which they did not know, for sure, who they were.

After years of slogging through documents and archives, I began to see my family heritage as a microcosm of the bone-deep conflicts in the history of Alabama, the Deep South, and the country itself. Yet now and then, amid all the information and note-taking, I'd find myself possessed of full-blown scenes from my childhood, which I called "bubbles of memory." Many of them came from that time with my mother during the war.

Slowly, those long-ago days began to shine like new gold in my mind as I saw how events were connected and how important that period had been to me. No matter what time of night or day a bubble appeared, I'd have to write it down—get out of bed and go to the computer, or grab the back of an envelope, or drive off the interstate into a McDonald's and write on that thin paper they put on your tray. Bit by bit, that long-banished time fell into place and put my mother back into the story of my life.

I think now of those precious wartime months as the gift

twice given. As a gift to my childhood, Momma's devotion at that time strengthened my sense of my own worth and enabled me to survive and go on without her. Forty years later, the memory of that gift—and the loss of it—brought her back to me in a way that could at last be shared and grieved.

Momma getting a parrot to talk. Momma at the kitchen table teaching me my part in a play. Momma scrubbing Knoxie's apartment and packing the trunks.

I remember. I had a mother. She loved me.

The Last
Happy Day of Her Life

· ·

CHERYL PEARL SUCHER

It was four o'clock in the morning, and I was alone, huddled beneath a white cotton blanket on a reclining chair in the darkened waiting room of Columbia Presbyterian Hospital's Neurological Intensive Care Unit, afraid to sleep. The hallway was empty but for a janitor waxing the tile floor. I had just sent my New Zealand fiancé home (our engagement was still a secret) so he could get some rest, and I was waiting for the ward nurse to call me in to say good-bye to my mother. I was determined to be with her when she passed. I did not want her to be alone. For her entire life, she had never been alone. She had survived the Plaszow ghetto, Ravensbrück, and Bergen-Belsen concentration camps with the support of her mother, my Bubbah. They lived together after the liberation, and my Bubbah moved in with my parents after they married in Lübeck in 1948, where she lived with them until her death thirty years later.

My mother suffered the first of her sudden paralyses and strokes, whose accumulation would ultimately be diagnosed as multiple sclerosis, when she was only thirty years old and my Bubbah was round-the-clock by her bedside. After my Bubbah died, my mother, then confined to a wheelchair, was cared for by a series of robust, maternal Polish housekeepers who cleaned, cooked, and tended house as they bathed and dressed her, becoming her constant companions.

In 1982, my mother lost the use of her arms following complex surgery to remove her left kidney and insert a bladder stoma. The eight-hour operation left her a quadriplegic suffering from chronic itches that tormented her. She had to be fed, turned, dressed, bathed, scratched, and changed. Her caretaker was not equipped to handle the challenge and my father reluctantly placed an ad in the Polish newspaper for a housekeeper/caretaker, because he didn't want to put her in a medical facility. A hard-bitten, chain-smoking middle-aged woman named Regina Czarnowska from Ostrowenka, who had been a social worker in her native land, answered the advertisement. Tough, strong, and shrewd, "Krisha" would care for my mother for seventeen years, until the very end, sleeping in my mother's bedroom, working seven days a week with only an occasional holiday, employing young Polish medical students and drivers to sustain my mother's care when her lungs failed and she was put on a respirator a year after my father's death in 1993.

Krisha was not with me that night because she could not bear to watch my mother die. She had become the conduit of my mother's emotions and communications, the arbiter of her wishes, her arms and her legs. When I was suffering from the flu, Krisha would drive to my apartment in their specially fitted wheelchair van with homemade chicken soup. When I cried about a man I loved—a non-Jew who was intolerable to my father—Krisha told me that my mother's heart broke for me, and that she had tried to convince my father to accept our relationship, but his will was too strong. (At the time, my father told me that he would have accepted him but for my mother.) Now that my father was gone, my mother spoke for herself, through Krisha.

The irony was my mother became a mother to me only after my father and Bubbah were no longer around to run interference. From infancy, my Bubbah had been like an offensive guard protecting my mother, the quarterback, from a sacking. If I was upset about something, my Bubbah insisted that I not tell my mother, for my woes would surely make her sicker. My father played the role of both parents to me and also became my best friend.

I saw my mother as the ethereal figure on the sofa, smoking her evening cigarette, watching television, playing mah-jongg. Whenever she fell, time stopped. She would cry like a trapped

animal and only my father could pick her up. If my grandmother and I were alone with her, we would have to call the
neighbors. When I was an adolescent and she would fall, I
would try to get her back into her wheelchair on my own,
but my attempts to get her to sit straight only caused her
more pain.

For most of my life, I resented my mother and the illness
that became the center of our family. Everything revolved
around her needs. I hated the sound of her cane preceding
her slow step as she came to wake me up every morning singing "Good Morning to You!" in her high-pitched soprano. I
could not look at her stubborn legs with their medical scars,
her clubbed feet in their shapeless orthopedic shoes, and
the paralyzed hand that curled into her body like a dying
petal. But her face was as lovely as ever — heart-shaped with
pomegranate lips and dark eyes crowned by perfectly peaked
brows and a full head of jet-black hair.

THAT NIGHT AT the hospital thirteen years ago, my
mother existed in the twilight realm between dream and
consciousness. Her doctors had summoned me there earlier,
explaining that even though her electroencephalograms were
registering violent electrical activity, she remained in a deep
coma. They wanted to know if my brother and I would approve taking her off the powerful drugs that were elevat-
ing her blood pressure because they were beginning to cause

damage to her vital organs. When we asked if she might regain consciousness, the consulting neurologist replied that he had seen such mysterious brain activity only once before, in another patient as chronically ill as my mother. It was his intuition that this wild, inexplicable mental tumult was the way her functioning mind was detaching from consciousness. These ineluctable brain seizures, he explained, were marking her mysterious transition from life to death.

At her bedside, I saw that her lips were encrusted with pus and her limbs swollen like pupae from the total failure of her renal pathways. I thought about how she had always been the first person to call and sing happy birthday to me — and then she would say, in a wistful tone of voice, that the day that I was born was the last happy day of her life. This was no exaggeration, for she had suffered that first series of strokes three months after my birth. Rushed to the hospital, she was completely paralyzed except for the movement of her left eye. Sustained by an iron lung, her condition worsened. The paralysis was traveling through her body, approaching her brain stem. To stop its course, her physicians asked my father's permission to intravenously administer an experimental drug that was so strong they gave it only to those they were sure would die. My father consented, gathering around her closest friends and family as he expected her to pass that night. It was an unspeakable tragedy. She was only thirty-one years old. She miraculously survived, but a spidery scar remained on the inside of her left calf, a souvenir of the powerful drug's work. For the forty years left of her life, her blood pressure plunged to zero three more times. Each time, she came home from the hospital, defying the prognoses of her physicians.

But now my mother was not rallying. I had been preparing for her death for weeks, as she had been exhibiting a decreasing interest in life, similar to my father's behavior in the weeks before he died. When I visited her, she was despondent, no longer animated, and more often asleep than awake. She refused food and had difficulty swallowing. All the activities that used to bring a smile to her face now brought no reaction. She didn't want to go to the boardwalk in Long Beach to inhale the sea air or eat a chocolate Danish or even talk about her love for my father and our frequent family jaunts to Atlantic City. She wasn't even asking about Charlie and Sara, her beloved grandchildren. When I held her hand, it was without weight or resistance. I knew that she was letting go.

My brother and I approved the withdrawal of all drugs as well as her feeding tube. She would receive only a glucose drip to make her comfortable. But we didn't know what to do about her respirator. If we detached her from the machine that had been breathing for her for over six years, she would die immediately. After discussing it, we decided to let it continue to breathe for her because it was the respirator that had kept her alive long enough to witness the birth of both her grandchildren. Then I started to shake the way I shook when my father was taken by ambulance to the hospital for the last time. I knew that there would be no more remarkable resurrection returns from the dead.

Since my father's death, I was in the habit of visiting my mother every Saturday or Sunday afternoon. No matter what my life's disappointments, she always said that my goodness and strength would ultimately be rewarded with love, success, and joy. During those weekend visits, Krisha would prepare an elaborate lunch and afterward we would retire to the den and watch ice-skating or golf, which we found soothing as background. My mother watched television constantly. It kept her from going mad. In those few hours, I would hold her hand and she would talk incessantly, letting go of all the thoughts and fears and questions that had accumulated during the week. In her darkest despair, she would rail about the tragedy of her illness, and a few times she even asked me to contact Dr. Kevorkian so she could end her life. When she was depressed, she was furious, and the tremors that beset her paralyzed limbs would increase in vigor and intensity. Her hands would go rigid and her face would freeze in an expression of fear and despair. But mostly, she was relaxed and happy to see me, reminiscing about what a good husband my father had been, how he had always looked after her and treated her like a queen. I did not contradict her, though I knew that my father often blamed his fate on her illness. The mythology of my father deepened in those weekend reminiscences. After his death, their marriage was perfect, and I did not dare challenge that notion.

My mother always asked me about myself, and if I had heard from any of the members of our small, extended family. Periodically, she would cough and choke and seize, and the respirator would start beeping. The Polish technician would run in, unpack a pair of powdered plastic gloves and clear the phlegm out of her lungs with a suction machine and plastic tubing. It was always painful and she hated it. But when she was wheeled back into the room, she would pick up our conversation. As her years on the respirator accumulated, she spent more and more time with oxygen infused into her breath, humidity added to ease the coarse flow of air.

She rarely complained, even when they pounded her back to release the phlegm, which was often thick as concrete. Sometimes she would ask me to scratch her nose, wipe her eyes. I'd make her laugh by taking the tweezers out of a nearby drawer to pull a whisker out of her chin. "You're getting to look like a hillbilly!" I would say.

"Cheryl, the day after you get married is when I'll die."

"Stop talking nonsense."

"There is a bank account I created just for your wedding."

I thought she was being playful. My mother had always been generous with gifts, as it was the only way she could express her love for her family. When my first novel was published after years and years of struggle, she sent me two dozen long-stemmed roses. She bought me my first set of pearls and surprised me with the gifts of my first laptop computers.

"Don't talk about that now, Mom," I said, sure that when and if I got married, we would share the experience. "We'll get big strong men to lift you up in your wheelchair when we dance the hora," I told her, laughing, rubbing moisturizer on her face, caressing her cheek. She would smile and shake her head wistfully, implying that was her final statement on the matter.

My mother met John Macready, my Kiwi fiancé, the previous Rosh Hashanah. I had brought him to our family meal, and he approached her in a way that most people did not once she was on the respirator. Somehow the mechanism of the speaker as well as the continuing drone of the breathing machine made most people treat her like she was one of the mechanical devices keeping her alive. They maintained their distance, talking at her rather than making the effort of listening to her, speaking to Krisha and the caretakers, rarely to her. But when my fiancé met her, he held the speaker to her throat, crouching down to hear her better, asking questions that she could barely answer because, by this time, she was weak and tired. Though our engagement was still a secret, I think she knew that he was the one. Somehow she realized that I was not going to be alone.

My mother did not pass that night, but lived in the hospital for two more weeks. Krisha finally came to visit after I relayed to her the words of my mother's kind Filipino nurse who suggested that my mother was holding on because she needed to say good-bye to her best friend.

When Krisha emerged from my mother's hospital room, she handed me a piece of paper—a bank statement.

"Your mother made me promise that I would show this to you before she died," she said. It was a savings account in trust to me. "Since your father's death, she has been depositing a monthly sum for you. It's for your wedding."

The amount was substantial. My mother now knew that there would be someone to love and watch over me, the same way that my father had loved and watched over her.

"You know, Krisha," I said, "if John were Jewish, she might have held on just a little bit longer." We held each other, laughing and weeping.

My mother died on Shabbos, when the purest souls are said to go directly to heaven. Less than a year later, twelve years ago, I married John at a hotel in New York City, on the hottest day of the last century. My mother had left me enough money to invite everyone I cared about to a lavish ceremony and reception, and to take a dream honeymoon in Italy. The celebration she had always wished that we would share was held in her honor. John and I toasted her gift to us as I told my guests that I hoped that my mother and father were dancing together in heaven, where all good souls go to rest.

Never Too Late

ABIGAIL POGREBIN

When I was growing up, my mother, Letty, always sewed elaborate Halloween costumes for me, cheered my every softball game and musical revue, and even helped me win first prize in the "Original Hat" contest at Fire Island's day camp when she sent me with a colander cap filled with sea grass sticking out of every hole. Every Hanukkah, she bought a present for each of us three kids for each of the eight nights, and her holiday tables were something to anticipate and ogle—festooned with candles, crystal, honey, and challah.

But her most memorable gift to me was the flowers. The flowers for my bat mitzvah at age forty. The fact that she suggested them, insisted she pay for them, and found a florist who transformed what would otherwise have been a grim space into a fantasyland, is the gift I'll remember most about her. My mother gave me the flowers that in turn gave me one of the rare flawless days of my life.

Once I decided I was going to become a bat mitzvah, I had to find a synagogue. I didn't belong to one and you can't just schedule a bat mitzvah in any synagogue if you don't pay dues. Neither can you plop your makeshift service in any JCC or YMCA because your space needs a Torah and a Torah is expensive to rent and unlikely to find. Do you know anyone who happens to have a Torah scroll in his closet?

The young rabbi, Jennifer Krause, who had been teaching me Judaism 101 for three years (and who gave me the idea to do this belated bat mitzvah thing in the first place), didn't have a pulpit, so there was no natural shul or hall to land in. I did occasionally attend the Upper West Side hub of Conservative Judaism—B'nai Jeshurun—on the High Holy Days, but I didn't consider myself a real congregant.

So, after much hand-wringing, and with my husband's nudge and blessing, I finally decided to plunk down more money than I'd anticipated to rent an old synagogue that now functions as an event space: Angel Orensanz, located on Norfolk Street on the Lower East Side of Manhattan. (Sarah Jessica got married there.) I liked that it was dusty, dimly lit, and historical. I liked that it was a raw space to make our own. And of course, they had the essential prop: a Torah in the ark.

The date was set, the space was booked, the Hebrew was (almost) memorized, but I wasn't sure how the day would actually come to life. I hadn't planned on any set pieces or lighting that would guarantee "the magic" and didn't know where it would come from on its own.

And then Mom said, out of the blue: "I want to contribute the flowers."

At first I wasn't sure what she meant.

"You mean a bouquet or two?"

"I always regretted that I didn't give you a bat mitzvah," she confessed. "For all the reasons that I was wrestling with Judaism personally during your childhood, I decided to take your bat mitzvah off the table. And so you didn't learn anything. And that milestone passed without a service or celebration. There is no getting that day back. So I want to get you the flowers for your bat mitzvah. That's the least I can do now."

I can't say I was entirely sure why I'd decided to go through with this ritual. A bar or bat mitzvah is supposed to be the day a child becomes a Jewish adult and, God knows, I'd passed the adult demarcation decades ago. I was also somewhat embarrassed about all the Jewish education I'd never had, let alone mastered, so I wasn't in a hurry to trumpet my ignorance with a ceremony.

But when Jennifer suggested the idea, something tugged at

me. I didn't like what I didn't know. I regretted what I'd never learned. This was a chance to catch up, to connect to something enduring—to choose a tradition I don't remember ever being given the chance to embrace or reject. The three years I'd spent unpacking lines of Bible verse with Jennifer and my good friend Jamie Lynton had been galvanizing somehow. Without any expectation of being moved or feeling spiritual, simply the exercise of studying a few lines or chapters with a smart rabbi had deepened the world for me, made me read fiction differently, see movies differently, hear lyrics differently, look anew at beautiful views. There was an electricity in study, which no one had forecast, an ineffable power in the weekly conversation itself. The more I learned, the more I wanted to know, the more I felt.

And then Jennifer said, "You should go further. You should take the next step." And before I knew it, we were starting to plan and prepare. She gave me recordings of her voice to help me memorize the complete Shema and my Torah portion. I started writing (and rewriting) my d'var Torah— my minisermon—on the section of Torah that fell on my birthday, editing drafts upon drafts with Jennifer, and rehearsing out loud.

I began to consider the appropriate "afterparty"—a lunch for my family and friends (was I really inviting family and friends?)—that would happen somewhere near Angel Orensanz and hopefully not add too much to the price of the day. I kept feeling apologetic about this enterprise, like it was indulgent or silly somehow to plan a thirteen-year-old's party twenty-seven years later.

But my husband said, "We should host a nice lunch."

And then my mother said, "I'll do the flowers."

My mother, who was raised in an observant home in Queens and who became one of the rare bat mitzvahs of her day.

My mother, whose mother died of cancer when my mother was just fifteen, and who rejected her faith when she was excluded from the mourners' minyan solely because she was female.

My mother, who celebrated all the major Jewish holidays, but didn't return to true observance until she found a way to reconcile her Judaism with her feminism.

My mother, who constantly made us aware of her guilt and self-flagellation that she didn't give us a proper Jewish education like she had.

I asked her if she would chant Torah during my adult bat mitzvah and she said yes, and then panicked once she started practicing. "I'm too rusty," she said, sounding sad and stunned. "I wanted to do this for you but it's just too hard for me."

I said it was absolutely unimportant—it was—but I was aware she felt empty-handed, and I wasn't sure what to tell her I needed when I didn't know myself.

"I'll do the flowers," she announced, and I heard her spirits lift.

She hired her friend, Bella Meyer, a floral designer who has a soft face with twinkling eyes and Bohemian style. Meyer happens to be the granddaughter of Marc Chagall, which seemed no accident in the way she approached flowers: as artistic elements, colors on a palate. A graduate of the Sorbonne with a PhD in Medieval Art History, Bella came to meet us at Angel Orensanz and as she walked around the shadowed, cavernous hall, she asked what we envisioned and told us what she imagined.

But I couldn't imagine. I couldn't see how the space could be brightened, how she was going to create arrangements that would make much difference, frankly, let alone supply the warmth I knew in my gut was still missing.

I SLEPT AT my mother's house the night before the ceremony because supportive in-laws had lovingly descended upon our apartment with my husband and children for this event, and I knew I would be a stress-case.

When I arrived with my packed overnight bag at my childhood apartment, I went upstairs to my old room and found a card and a box. Mom had written a beautiful message about her astonishment and pride that I chose to do this myself. The green velvet box contained an engraved perfect silver Kiddush cup: ABBY 5-14-05.

I slept in my childhood room—the one that used to be decorated in the hunter green theme she'd let me select when

I was fourteen: Laura Ashley flowered wallpaper, cushioned headboard, quilt, orange telephone, butcher block desk. I remembered the stereo my parents received for free when they made a deposit at the local bank—it had built-in disco lights that flashed to the beat of my eight-track tapes. I recalled the sound of the traffic down below in winter—which I'm still convinced has a different sound than traffic in summer.

My mother kissed her forty-year-old daughter good night and I tried to sleep.

The next morning, a stunning May Saturday, we rode the subway together in heels down to Essex Street. I carried the wine and bread for the Kiddush blessings, plus the customized prayer books, yarmulkes, candlesticks, and matches. My father had given me the tallis he was married in. I don't think he'd worn it since.

When we walked up the dilapidated stairs of Angel Orensanz and entered the sanctuary, I gasped. Bella had created the equivalent of Willy Wonka's chocolate factory. There were purples and whites and reds and pinks, cascading and exploding everywhere. The room was a forest and an oasis. It felt like jewels had been strung and music was playing.

I hugged my mother and kept saying thank you. For the first time, I exhaled and knew what I was there to do. To hold something close and keep something safe. To honor what my mother had inherited and, for her own reasons, couldn't pass on before today. Now she was ready to give it to me (and so relieved I had arrived here in time for her to see it). Her atonement and reinforcement was visible—even fragrant—in the peonies, daffodils, and lilacs.

THE CEREMONY IS a blur and also utterly crystalline. I recall my father placing his tallis around my shoulders. I recall my parents' aliyah and my husband's. I won't forget reading the Torah in front of me—the magnitude of the words I was looking at, that the letters were each handcalligraphed, that so many had died to keep reading them, to protect them, that this code no longer appeared foreign to me.

I remember delivering my d'var Torah in a steady voice, looking out at the faces I knew so well, and smelling the flowers as if their scent alone was there to hold me up and guide me to the finish line.

Most powerful of all, I recall my children's blessings over the candles, bread, and wine. Ben was eight and Molly six. They looked like freshly scrubbed angels, and their little voices made me feel blessed.

We all exited the murky hall into spring sunlight. My friends walked, chatting, down the street to the corner of Norfolk and Delancey—finding seats in the breezy little Italian café that was waiting for us, its doors opened to the sidewalk. The tables were long banquet-style, twinkling with plates and glasses, and Bella's flowers dancing down the center. Mom had asked her to make the lunch beautiful, and that's the only word for how it all looked: beautiful. I hadn't known I could feel high from the sight of hydrangeas and lilies arranged in artful boxes.

My family and friends' speeches put me on a cloud. The food was delicious. The kids ran around with their cousins or spun around on the bar stools. My husband actually got choked up (a first) when he toasted me.

And in the midst of the joy were the flowers Mom bought me. They'd made the service feel transcendent. They'd made the lunch exuberant and elegant at the same time. She gave me more in those gusts of color and vegetation than I could even have imagined.

My mother didn't give me Judaism when maybe she should have, but she made up for it.

Thank you for the roses, Mommy.

The Broken Vase

· ·

REVEREND LILLIAN DANIEL

In her first international trip ever, my twenty-five-year-old mother moved from a small town in South Carolina to Tokyo, when I was just six months old. There we met my father, a foreign correspondent who had taken one day to pick out a house for us in a traditional Japanese neighborhood. A stylish Southerner with a taste for adventure, bouffant hairdos, and high-heeled shoes, my mother soon learned how to speak the language, to bathe standing up, and to collect Asian pottery. As our family went on to move from one country to another, my parents grew their collection of pottery. Since the pieces were arranged around the house just out of reach of running children and frisky dogs, it was not until I was a teenager that I noticed a vase that did not fit with the rest of the collection.

With a cream glaze and a blue Japanese design, it looked like it had once been a fine antique, but now it was badly damaged and glued together. It stood amid the finer pieces, a mass of cracks crudely bound with what was obviously the wrong type of adhesive — everywhere the twenty or so pieces met, glue had bubbled out yellow as it dried, creating the effect of scabrous scars, or a dried-up runny nose.

"Why don't you get rid of that one?" I asked my mother. "It looks just awful next to the others."

"Never," she replied. "It's the most valuable piece of pottery we have in this house."

Then she told me the story.

WHEN I WAS a toddler, my journalist father covered the Vietnam War, moving in and out of the war zone for weeks at a time. Whenever he returned home, he brought a piece of Asian pottery to add to my mother's collection. The vase was one of the finest he'd found, and he wrapped it in brown paper and string and carried it carefully on several airplanes and buses before finally walking up the driveway with it in his hands.

That was the moment I, at two years old, saw him and rushed forward. Surprised and elated, my father opened his arms. As I fell into them, the vase fell out and smashed into pieces. My father gasped, but my mother had no concern for the broken vase; she was just delighted to see me in my daddy's arms. Later that night, my mother pulled out the glue, clumsily repaired the vase, and pronounced it "precious."

It remains a symbol to me of why so many people loved her, and mourned her passing. There was no situation she didn't think could be repaired and redeemed, including her own illness. It surprised her by taking her from this world at the age of sixty.

She could always see the beauty in broken things, including in me. When I went through a brief stage at Yale Divinity School, attempting to adopt what I thought was the look of a serious student, in baggy linen dresses and stern glasses, she had to intervene. "Darling, it is wonderful that you want to be a minister," she said, "but I'll be damned if I will tolerate you dressing like a missionary." Most people who had known me as a teenager were shocked, perhaps appalled, to hear that I intended to go into the ministry. My mother claims that she had seen it coming. It seems she could often see things that other people couldn't; she did "makeovers" long before there was a word for it. Her friends were always showing up at our house with three suits on hangers, to ask my mother which one to wear to the job interview.

She saw the beautiful possibilities in everyone. So much so that whenever she'd tell me news about friends, she gave everyone a promotion. The medical resident became a chief surgeon, the teacher's assistant an assistant principle, and all were fascinating and successful. When her cultured-spiritual-but-not-religious friends were disdainful of my strange turn in career path, she defended my choice to lead a dying church where the small choir outnumbered the tinier congregation by telling her friends, "It's really very much like being a college president."

But when the reality of life hit hard, and failure crossed, my mother was somehow able to sweep away all those promotions and listen to people who doubted themselves with absolute attention. As a person who had failed herself in more than one arena—from some of her workplaces to her marriage—she was the kind of person you felt you could tell your failure story to and have it blessed. You could trust that she would see the beauty in broken things.

As a spiritual leader, I see my own calling very similarly. Until God gets around to the major repair work, as a person of faith, I try to repair the brokenness of the world in small ways. But ultimately, I have to learn to see the beauty, the image of God, in broken things, and to call them precious. These days, I strive to do all that as the senior minister at a large church in the wealthy suburbs of Chicago, where broken things are seldom displayed, but shunted out of sight, far back and behind the children's sports trophies and the smiling family portraits.

In Henry James's novel *The Golden Bowl,* the central metaphor that predicts the suffering of all the characters is a lovely bowl. But running through the bowl is a nearly invisible flaw that renders the treasure less valuable than it appears to be. The beautiful but flawed bowl mirrors the false contentment of the characters as they move about in desperation, in a society that has no room for flaws.

I've always hoped that the churches I serve can offer a different understanding of brokenness. When we gather around the communion table, the vessels, whether pewter plates or delicate chalices, are not the issue. It is in the breaking of the bread, tearing it out of the perfection of a formed loaf, and leaving the edges jagged, that we remember what Jesus said: "This is my body, broken for you." Those words render absurd our human preoccupation with perfection. True beauty comes, not from the flawless piece, nor from the piece that pretends to have no crack.

On the Sunday mornings when I preside at the communion table, I tell the congregation that our salvation lies in God's broken body. But in real life, as I lead a complex organization, I am not so different from any other leader. I fall prey to the same pressures, and the same ambitions. I want my church to be perfect. So in the frenetic pace of children's classes, choir rehearsals, efforts to create more programs and attract more people, a congregation and its minister can forget the beauty of being broken, and appear to be a congregation without flaw or fault. In my suburban village, where our idolatry is not so much the golden calf but that other graven image, "the perfect family," perfection in the church can have heartbreaking and isolating results. When happily married, a family attends church, but once divorced, they wonder if they still belong. At his wife's funeral, the grieving widower finds peace in the sanctuary, but on Sunday morning, the church seems to be a place with too much cheerful veneer to make room for his scars.

My mother's great gift of seeing the beauty in broken things pushes me to push my church to resist the culture of the golden bowl. When we can acknowledge the beauty of the broken vase, remarkable things can happen. The hungry are fed, the homeless sheltered in the midst of affluence, and personal testimony moves from victory dance to truth telling.

Yet order and flawlessness are seductive in a chaotic world. One evening, years after my mother had died, my father sat at my long clean kitchen counter, littering it with an explosion of newspapers, magazines, coffee cups — all teetering on the edge of chaos. When he gestured to call my attention to an article he was reading, the coffee cup went flying, spilling onto the papers in a sticky mess and breaking when it hit the floor.

"I'll get it," he said, using a magazine as a mop.

"No, Dad, it's OK," I said, in a tone that indicated it might be time for him to leave. "I'll clean it up after you're gone."

AFTER HE LEFT I picked up the pieces of the broken coffee cup, mopped up the papers, and pulled out the spray-on cleaner. As the fumes of disinfectant hit my nose and the counter shone once again, I breathed a sigh of relief.

That was the last time he drank coffee at our counter. I could not have known that I should have paid more attention that night, worried less about the mess, and perhaps had him stay awhile longer. Today my counter sparkles, but I want the mess back. I want to see the sticky rim of a coffee cup, mop up newspapers read and discussed and stamped with a date of a happier day.

Now that my father is gone, I preside at another unfinished meal. I stand at the communion table where my brokenness finds its place in the open arms of Jesus, and my eyes are opened in the breaking of the bread. Clean counters, golden bowls, and perfect people are no match for the broken vase that now sits on a grown orphan's mantel. Its beauty lies in the scars themselves, reminders that over the generations, God has picked us up, put us back together, placed us back on the best shelf and called us precious.

My MOTHER WAS a magnificent entertainer. There was something about a meal at her house that topped everything, though it was not necessarily the cooking. Sometimes that was delicious, but other times, the gravy might have burned on the stove, or the chicken was frighteningly undercooked, or the whole meal came out an hour late, blackened and crunchy— including the green beans. But there was something about being at that table that pointed you toward abundance. You knew you were special, that someone had set the table for you, put on festive music, and killed the fatted calf, even if the food was strange. There were always flowers and candles. My mother had a keen sense of both her strengths and her limitations as a hostess. Her entertaining motto was, "Well, it may not be good, but it'll certainly be fancy."

One night, she came out of the kitchen more than an hour late, dressed to the nines in a sparkly outfit a couple of sizes too small, red high-heeled shoes clicking across the floor, and she was holding—on another giant Japanese pottery tray—a magnificent roasted duck. It was a brand new recipe for her. We had waited a long time for the meal, but it was hard to see the duck on the plate, for in her enthusiasm for her project, she had gone heavy on the garnish. It was like a parsley explosion of culinary enthusiasm, a product of a long day's work, cheerfully given. But then, the combination of all the greenery, the grease of the duck, and a fold in the carpet just underneath her high-heeled shoes all came together in the perfect storm. As she tripped, the duck she had spent the whole day preparing went flying across the room. The bird landed where once it had had its tail feathers and skidded across the floors, only to stop on the muddy doormat in the front hall, a brown trail of grease, gravy, and parsley garnish in its sad wake.

The hostess had a moment where tears welled up, and

there was a collective gasp among the guests. You could see that my mother was thinking about how she would be judged. She knew from experience how easily people mock a woman of enthusiasm when her big plans go wrong. But then, as if a new spirit came upon her, she pulled her little shoulders back and marched over to the defeated duck on the doormat. As she stooped down and picked it up, she announced to the group, "Let me just throw this duck away in the kitchen, and I'll be back in just a minute with the other duck."

A few minutes later, she made another grand entrance, this time avoiding the crease in the carpet, and this time with a duck even more heavily disguised in garnish, to cover the bruises, for of course, as we all knew, there was no other duck. But the holy spirit of hospitality was such that without a word, it was as if the guests collectively decided to replace the world's petty practices of judgment and critique with a spirit of generosity. And we sinners all ate well at the table that night, feasting less on the damaged duck than on the grace that was served to both an embarrassed hostess and to her hungry guests.

This remains my vision of the heavenly banquet, my hope for the life that is to come. I imagine my mother greeting me with a plate of burnt hors d'oeuvres. I imagine my father relaxing at the table, with the cup of coffee he never got to finish at my counter. And there with my parents is the original artist who made us all, the one who delights in broken things and calls them precious.

The Wok

....

CECILIA MUÑOZ

My mother spent months looking for the right wok for me. It had to be lightweight, because of my carpal tunnel syndrome, and it had to be well made, because my mother was a connoisseur of kitchen tools—not to mention a world-class cook. I don't know if the fact that she was so sick made her search take longer; the wok was the last birthday present she gave me before she died in 2008, after eighteen years with cancer. The care she took in finding it is one of the reasons it's so special to me—one of many reasons.

I use it often to make quick meals for my husband and daughters—with the emphasis on *quick*. Having had more-than-full-time jobs all my working life, time for leisurely cooking has always been in short supply. My husband uses the wok, too, but we both consider it mine, considering the source. We know that my mother wanted me to have a wok because she knew it would help me feed my family on my terms, which are so different from the way she fed *her* family—my father and four kids *and,* on nearly every holiday, the dozens of relatives whom she welcomed into our house in suburban Detroit.

We were then an extended network of immigrants from Bolivia, who had begun coming to the United States in the 1950s. My mother's extraordinary hospitality—illuminated by her cooking and her elegant presentation—helped transform us from a band of outsiders to Americans with roots here, and deep connections to one another. There was always room for one more, one more son sent from Bolivia to finish growing up, one more cousin, one more new husband or wife. Sometimes there were forty people at Thanksgiving dinner. There were tables everywhere for those who didn't fit in the dining room, each with a floral or ceramic centerpiece, each one attempting to be an elegant miniature of the "grown-up" table, a mahogany replica of my father's parents' table, sent in crates from Bolivia.

On ordinary days, my mother began cooking at 3:30—and dinner was ready every day at 5:35, exactly five minutes after my father came through the door whistling, home from his job as an engineer at Ford Motor Company. The food was on the table, and there were formal rules, including napkins on laps, elbows off the table. Yes, there were rules—but what all of us remember, what all of us learned, was the art of conversation. We talked about politics, science, music, and literature. We talked about homework, class work, and we shared math problems. For years the talk was way over my head, as the youngest, but once I caught up, I wasn't afraid to enter the fray. The night one of my brothers brought a logic question to the table and I figured it out, I felt very smart and grown-up.

Far from just feeding us and decorating the table, my mother was an avid participant in the conversations. She was a voracious reader, especially of history and archaeology—passions which she and my younger daughter shared from early on. My mother was so intellectually engaged, my siblings kept encouraging her to go to college, but she was busy and intimidated by not being able to write well in English. She spoke beautifully and had a great vocabulary, but never felt comfortable putting pen to paper in her adopted language; I have only one letter she ever sent me in English. When her children went to college, in our enthusiasm for the bright new world we were entering, we wanted the same for her and felt disappointed that she didn't want to pursue the education we felt she deserved, but my mother seems to have made peace with it. I don't think she felt sad for herself in the same ways that we felt sad for her.

As a young woman in Bolivia, she had looked like Ingrid Bergman, and had had many suitors. She chose my father— not the most glamorous of them—because he gave her serious books to read and liked to talk to her. They married in 1950, when she was twenty, and journeyed north for an unglamorous honeymoon in Ann Arbor, Michigan, so my father could complete a single course credit for the engineering degree at the University of Michigan, which he attended during World War II. (His father had taken a master's in engineering at Michigan in the 1920s, and raised his family in Bolivia to sing the U. of M. fight song, and to admire his photograph of the football stadium.)

My parents planned to stay in the United States for a year, but when they were about to return to Bolivia, their families told them to wait: there were no jobs; the political situation was bad. In 1952, there was a revolution. By 1957, my three siblings had been born, my father had a good job, and they owned a house. They still planned to go home, but when they talked about it soon after I was born in 1962, they realized that they had become Americans. There was no turning back.

By then, my mother had become quite an accomplished cook—and would eventually become a successful saleswoman. She hadn't known much about the kitchen when she married, but as a newlywed and young mother, she read cookbooks and magazines, listened to radio cooking shows, and learned by trial and error. Oysters Rockefeller, Julia Child's duck *à l'orange,* the Bolivian dishes she'd grown up with—there was very little she couldn't do. Before she started to work, she minded us, and took classes in cake decorating and hat making to stave off boredom — that was how she explained those courses to me.

A few years after I was born, she took a bold step out of the house and began a career that would change my parents' circumstances considerably. She sold cosmetics for a company that rivaled Avon. She arranged for women to hold sales parties in their houses. And she was incredibly successful — as competent in that world as she was in the kitchen. So competent that in the 1970s, she was selling five thousand dollars a month of makeup — enough to qualify for a company car, which became our family's second car. It allowed my parents to send two siblings to private colleges (my sister and I followed our father, uncles, and grandfather to U. of M.), and allowed my parents to travel the world. My mother loved her independence, and loved being able to make a contribution to the family. In addition to working intensively, making makeup deliveries on the way back from my music lessons, and leaving for makeup parties after dinner, she still had dinner for six on the table every day at 5:35, and she still entertained legions of relatives for nearly every holiday — including birthdays and anniversaries.

ALL OF THIS and more comes back to me in those early mornings when I find myself doing laundry for my family before I go to work: my mother's phenomenal cooking, her success in business, memories of her scrubbing the kitchen floor late at night. I used to wonder why she waited until so late.

Now I don't have to wonder. "That's what she was doing," I say aloud, as though it's fresh news every time. She was doing it all.

I know I have had advantages my mother never had—ones she never dreamed of—among them an education, a series of "important" jobs that keep me working more than full-time, and a husband who cooks, cleans, and has always taken regular care of our children, taking them to the doctors, music lessons, and play dates. My mother, a paragon of generosity, was always happy for me, proud of my work, proud of the success I've had. She never said what part of me always feared she would say: "Why don't you spend more time tending your family, your kitchen, your garden, your house the way I did?" Instead she overlooked the relative chaos of my household and said, "I admire how you manage to do your work and still be a good mother." And I think she meant it.

But one thing I've had to live with that has been both an advantage and, at times, a burden, is her example as a homemaker. She has been both an inspiration and a hard act to follow. Her model showed me how to be "the perfect wife and mother," or perhaps I mean, "the perfect wife and mother for her generation." My sister and I—like most women our age—have had to invent new ways of being wives and mothers, only to find that the new ways have a great deal in common with the old ways.

Because of my mother's magnificent example, putting food

on the table has never been the only goal of the evening meal: it's where we connect, where we teach our children to converse, where we settle at the end of the day to remind ourselves that we are a family, and that this connection matters. We're together until we scatter soon after for nightly tasks: homework, housework, reading, and bedtime.

My mother *was* a hard act to follow as a homemaker, but the gift of the wok is one of many gifts from her that have made my life as rich as it is. This simple pan, unconnected to our family's origins, usually sits in our cupboard and allows me to stir-fry vegetables, tofu, and savory spices in delicious, healthy combinations—and do it quickly, in a matter of minutes—so I can juggle the two most important pieces of my life, my family and my career, just a little more easily. My mother knew that the wok would help me do that. But she could never have known that I would treasure the wok as I do, because it reminds me of her thoughtfulness, and because it opens the door to so many memories—so many lessons in creating and sustaining the connections that matter most.

How They Do It in France

....

ELISSA SCHAPPELL

When I moved into my first apartment twenty-some odd years ago, my mother, an inspired, marvelous cook, gave me one of her cake pans. It was round, its once-nonstick bottom cross-hatched with silver scratches. It wasn't pretty. I'd have thrown it out, if I hadn't needed it.

When I look at the pan, I can imagine my mother — perhaps with a bit of paint in her hair from a new still life she'd been working on, or breathless from picking up me and my sister from a gymnastics class — delicately attempting to remove a sponge cake from the pan, and failing to do so with the sort of grace and ease she desired, scraping the bottom of the pan.

For my mother — despite the fact that she cooked all the time, for us and regularly for dinner guests, entertaining them with exotic dishes like Mongolian hot pot and cassoulet; despite the fact that she was co-owner of a boutique catering business that specialized in high-end hors d'oeuvres and fancy foods—my mother is not a fabulous baker.

Growing up I assumed that every coconut cake leaned forward like a stout opera singer mid-aria, that every chocolate layer cake was propped up or held together with a series of girderlike toothpicks. It never occurred to me that the ring of pachysandra around the Black Forest cake disguised the fact that there was a hole in the side. I didn't realize that you didn't routinely cut the bottom off a cake. Wasn't that just part of the process? I believed there were cookies that were meant to be overbaked, because they were best that way with tea, and others underbaked because they were fun to mold with your hands.

It wasn't until I got a little older, when I started going to other kids' houses, that I discovered the truth. My friends' mothers' cakes weren't constructed with a vast system of beams and joists. There were no tunnels in the center of their birthday cakes, no burnt aftertaste, no masses of ivy and roses, literally, bringing up the rear. And, I felt a little jealous. A little embarrassed.

When I asked my mother why we couldn't just *buy* a cake, like normal people, she'd looked confused, shocked, as though buying a cake not only reflected a lack of imagination, but a lack of care. It was so impersonal.

When I got my own apartment and started cooking and baking, it became clear that I'd inherited my mother's recessive Betty Crocker gene. Even so, when I threw a birthday party for a dear friend, I felt I had to bake him a cake. It had burned, and not only that, the collateral damage from my attempts to remove it from the pan was pretty horrific. I didn't have time to run out and purchase a cake.

"It's not a problem," my mother said when I called her in tears. "Just cut off the bottom."

"I can't do that."

"Yes you can. You just tell your guests, 'That's how they do it in France.'"

My mother laughed, as though she'd said this a million times.

"No," I said, "I'll just tell him the truth. I'll apologize profusely and . . ."

"No, you will not," she said firmly. "Just cut off the bottom and use a lot of frosting, do you have pecans? Cover it in nuts, or confectioners' sugar. Put it on a pretty plate, do you have any flowers? It's all in the presentation."

I could do that. I *had* inherited a beautiful Victorian glass cake stand from my grandmother, and some bone china dishes painted with violets. I did have some baby's breath from the five-dollar bouquet of flowers I'd picked up at the corner market.

"Then simply pick up your chin, smile, and serve it with pride. Just say, 'This is how they do it in France.'"

I thought about it. Didn't people rave about my mother's cooking, even her desserts, praising her creativity? I recalled a fallen angel food cake, less than heavenly on the plate, covered in pureed frozen raspberries and served in the antique glass compotes from my grandmother. It was one of my favorite desserts.

I'D ALWAYS SWORN that when I became a mother, I would buy cakes for my children—how I had longed for a store-bought cake with lifelike roses and *Happy Birthday* written in elegant cursive, versus herky-jerky capitals. A cake with smooth-as-glass icing, delicately accented with silver balls and lifelike pink roses. Not a cake cratered as the moon, encrusted with rainbow jimmies. And as I attended a parade of fancy parties, more like wedding showers than birthday parties—the guest of honor's likeness airbrushed onto a triple-decker cake—it became clear that I was not up to the task. My baking would only bring shame on my family. However, when the time was upon me—when I needed a birthday cake to honor my child—I wavered.

Instead, my son and daughter would, and always will, get the cakes they ask for. A pink caterpillar, its unsightly lumps and bumps disguised with "spines and bristles" (toothpicks topped with baby marshmallows), and long candles. A scooter, which, thanks to my impatience liberating the sheet cake from the pan, will look like a cracked gravestone on wheels. A castle painstakingly erected out of ladyfingers and crème that will, despite the popsicle buttresses and retaining wall of daisies wedged around it for stability, seconds after the camera's flash, begin to list, then slide and collapse, the victim, it seems, of an invisible landslide.

Guests will occasionally look perplexed, squint, and ask, "Is that a unicorn?" It is, or should be. But I can appreciate the species confusion. Clearly I've done a poor job of affixing the ears, and the horn is over-long.

I shrug. "It's a unicorn or a narwhal. Whatever suits your fancy."

My daughter grins, delighted. The narwhal's nickname is "the unicorn of the sea." And the guests will nod in a way that suggests they're just chalking it up to our being a little eccentric — and I suppose we are.

Here is what I have learned: Buy twice the amount of frosting to use as emergency Spackle. Sprinkles, colored sugar, M&M's, Rice Krispies, flaked coconut, gumdrops are your friends. Don't apologize. Remember the pan.

When I look at that banged-up pan, I think, *What matters is that you made the cake.* What mattered was that you served it with flair and spirit. What mattered was that the people you'd made it for felt you cared, and you did.

I suppose when my mother gave me that pan, she really gave me two gifts. Faith in me that I could make a cake and a philosophy for living one's life.

White Gloves
and Party Manners

· ·

KAREN KARBO

The book was an Easter present the year I turned eleven. It was propped on the white brick fireplace beside my white rattan Easter basket. A few neon yellow marshmallow Peeps perched atop the fat snarl of green plastic grass. There was also a hollow chocolate Easter bunny in a tall box with a cellophane window inside the basket. I remember that bunny distinctly—he was slightly melted, his head caved in a bit, his blue and yellow candy eyes cast heavenward like an ecstatic saint—and the book, *White Gloves and Party Manners*.

This was not my usual Easter book. At only sixty-five pages long, it was the size of a children's picture book. Usually the Easter book was an important hardback with a jewel-colored spine and beautiful illustrations. *The Wonderful Wizard of Oz.*

Alice in Wonderland. Tom Sawyer. On the cover was a line drawing of a girl with a soft side-parted pageboy and with puff sleeves, smocking across the chest, and a bow in back, the kind of loathsome dress my mom routinely gave my cousin and me for Christmas each year. I would get the blue one because I was a strapping hulk, and my cousin would get the pink one, since she was blond and petite. When I try to solve the riddle of my lifelong antipathy toward this cousin, the blue dress/pink dress tradition is as good an answer as any.

I remember sitting crossed-legged on the living room floor flipping through the pages of *White Gloves and Party Manners* with growing dismay. Inside, there were more delicate line drawings, not unlike those found in another book called *Very Personally Yours,* passed out during fifth-grade assembly when the girls were marched off to the cafeteria to receive the appalling news about menstruation.

The introduction explained that this was my first book about manners, and it would tell "what to do and what to say to make people like you." It promised that someday, "when you are a beautiful young lady, all dressed up in a flowing gown and long white gloves, you will be glad you read this book, because then you will be completely at ease, and have a wonderful time."

I closed the book and investigated the candy in my Easter basket. I would never be a beautiful young lady, all dressed up in a flowing gown and long white gloves, anywhere, ever. For one thing, I was already five feet eight. My mother had taken me to the pediatrician only a few months earlier to see if he had any advice about how she could safely stunt my growth. My shoulders were broad, my feet big, my hair, as my mother characterized it once to a hairdresser, like that of a Ubangi woman, and she had no idea where on earth that head of hair had come from.

My mother had been a stunning young woman, a real redhead with snowy skin, green eyes, and silky copper-penny-colored hair. She had been slim in all the places where I was wide. I realize I'm focusing exclusively on what she looked like, but during the time she was in my life, that was what we focused on. She believed a young lady's looks were money in the bank, something which her own experience had borne out.

She had grown up in the boardinghouse run by her mother, Maud Sharkey, in Ypsilanti, Michigan, a dozen miles east of Ann Arbor. She was the youngest of three sisters, and the most beautiful. Julia and Lorraine were twenty-two and twenty years older than her, respectively. They were short and round, with small pale blue eyes, large noses, tiny teeth, and tiny feet. They reminded me of a pair of nesting birds and were so different from my mother, who was tall and angular by comparison.

The Sharkey girls were working class, high school educated. Julia and Lorraine both married young. I don't know much about Julia's husbands — they kept dying and leaving her money—but Lorraine married a man named George who worked on the assembly line at Ford Motor Company, and they had a daughter, Mary. My mother did not marry young. She worked first as a secretary, then became the first female executive at Holley Carburetor Company; then, when she was twenty-five, she leveraged her beauty to snag my dad, who held a master's degree from Art Center School of Design (as it was then named) and worked in the design department at Ford. She had done what her sisters, and eventually her sisters' daughters, had failed to do: married up.

There's a lengthy section in *White Gloves and Party Manners* called "Meetings, Greetings and Good-byes," that teaches you what to say when you meet a congressman, a judge, an ambassador, a senator, and the vice president and president of the United States (and their wives). This is what she hoped for me, that, like her, I would grow from a gawky girl to a staggering beauty and climb the socioeconomic ladder a little higher.

She had her work cut out for her. I was tall and loud and spent a lot of my spare time whacking a tennis ball against the garage door. I was stubborn. I walked heavy and jiggled my legs when I ate. I liked to stand on my head in the living room. I asked for a unicycle one Christmas, and when my dad bought me one without consulting her, they had one of the only arguments I ever remember them having. In high school, I played every sport that would have me. I skateboarded and surfed. I had road rash on my knees, abrasions on my rib cage from the wax on my board, and muscular thighs that made my mother shake her head with genuine sorrow.

Even though it was the early '70s, the era of Helen Reddy's feminist anthem "I Am Woman," I believed my mother: my future depended on being a girly girl, on making sure boys thought I was smart but not too smart, sweet but not funny, receptive to the point of passivity. I spent hours straightening my unruly hair and trailing my mother through Bullock's and May Company, the department stores of my youth, in search of flattering clothes. Even though I wasn't overweight, but was merely tall and strong, we were perpetually on the hunt for skirts that were slimming, for tops that would minimize my broad shoulders. "You can do anything you set your mind to!" she once said. "If you want to make yourself over, you can."

My father had no such agenda. He was the only son of a self-made woman, Luna of California, as she called herself. They'd come from Warsaw to Chicago when my father was a boy. Somewhere along the way his father abandoned the family, and his mother moved them to Hollywood, where she parlayed sewing, her only real skill, into a business designing Christian Dior–inspired gowns for the wives of professional men and movie moguls. He believed my future would be more secure if I knew how to pound a nail, build a table, draw a box in perfect perspective, shoot a gun, change the oil in the car. The weekend after I got my driver's license he took me to an intensive three-day high-speed driving course, so I could really learn what a car could do. Like buying the unicycle, he did all this without consulting my mother, who believed that with each new skill I acquired, I was rendering myself less and less appealing. Once, when I was washing the car, down on my hands and knees scrubbing the white sidewalls with an old Brillo pad my father set aside for just that purpose, she came out and slapped the back of my head. "Stand up," she commanded, "This is men's work."

MY MOTHER WAS the only Sharkey sister in California, and so we spent that Easter, like every other Easter, with Lorraine's daughter, whom I called Aunt Mary, her husband, whom I called Uncle Dick, and their two children, Tim and Jeri. (To protect their privacy, let's call them the Mahoneys.) We spent every major holiday and all the minor ones with them, all the birthdays, anniversaries, and a lot of random Saturday nights. Over the Christmas holidays Lorraine and George, whom I called Gramma and Grandpa because Jeri and Tim called them Gramma and Grandpa, took the train from Detroit and stayed for six weeks, sometimes at our house, sometimes with the Mahoneys.

It was always the same: the adults would sit around in a circle smoking and balancing cocktails on their knees, silently negotiating some dark, complicated adult business I could sense but couldn't name. They would drink for hours, then my mom or Aunt Mary would "serve," as my mother called putting dinner on the table. My mother was a tremendous cook of the dishes of the time: beef Stroganoff, lasagna, spaghetti carbonara. Aunt Mary stuck with a hunk of meat, mashed potatoes, and an overcooked green vegetable. Often, when we ate at the Mahoneys', the drinking would go on too long and dinner would be late. Then there would be an argument. Aunt Mary would lose her temper and start screaming, my mom would try to talk her off the ledge, my dad would disappear into another room with a book, and Uncle Dick would go out to the backyard and drink straight from the bottle.

Because I was an only child, and Jeri had only a brother, we were encouraged to treat each other like sisters, but I couldn't force myself to like her. Her greatest crime that I could name—and did, when my mother begged me to be nicer—was that she never wanted to *do* anything, never wanted to ride bikes or play bike tag or statue maker. She didn't want to shoot baskets or hit the tennis ball against the garage door. Her preferred activity was sitting in her room at her pink vanity brushing her hair. When she was finally pressed into, for example, joining a neighborhood softball game, she would insist on being allowed to stay at bat until she hit the ball. If I protested, she'd take the matter to the adults. She would cry and I would glower and, somehow, I would be the one who wound up on the receiving end of a lecture.

Later, my mom would explain to me that when it came to my cousin Jeri, I had to be the bigger person because I had so many more advantages than she did. My father made more money than hers did, and I had nicer clothes. We lived in a nicer house in a nicer suburb. I was a superior girl in all ways, and because I was, I had to give Jeri a break. In this way my mom affirmed her basic premise, that if you were female, weak, and ineffectual, the rules would be bent for you, and in that way you would wind up the winner.

IN SOMEONE ELSE's story, the girl would leave home for college and all hell would break loose. The girl would embrace her wild hair, like the Jane Fonda character did in *Coming Home*. She'd drink too much, smoke pot, sleep around, and realize that her mother was pretty much full of shit, an opinion to be reversed when she, herself, became a mother, and saw how difficult and truly endless the task was.

Instead, three months after I arrived at the University of Southern California, when I was seventeen, my mother was diagnosed with brain cancer. She underwent an eight-hour surgery, during which the surgeon was able to remove some of the tumor, along with enough healthy brain tissue to completely change my mother's personality. Where she had loved cooking and parties and chatting on the phone with her friends for hours, she became moody and paranoid, convinced that my father and Gramma (her sister Lorraine), who had come to California on the train from Detroit to take care of her, were trying to kill her.

I was away at school, which is where my parents wanted me. They wanted me somewhere where they wouldn't have to worry about me, and also where I would be spared the horror of witnessing my mom's rapid decline. Three months after her surgery, I received a phone call on the house phone of the sorority house where I lived. It was my father, choking with tears. Lorraine took the phone from him and told me that my mother had slipped into a coma. While I was driving home from school, an ambulance took her to the hospital. I refused to go and see her in the ICU, an impertinence that earned me a slap across the face from Lorraine. I didn't see the point. If she was going to die, I didn't want this to be my final memory of her; if she somehow recovered, I would see her again when she wasn't in a coma. She died in the middle of the night, never having regained consciousness. I had turned eighteen the week before and had gone home for the occasion; it would be the last time I saw her. She was still on her feet. She'd spent the week before preparing my birthday dinner; it had taken her a day to set the table, moving slowly between the kitchen and the dining room, carrying one utensil at a time. The night of her funeral, I drove back to school and took an oceanography midterm. My father always liked to say that we Karbos were tough Polacks, and so we were. I got a B+ on the midterm. My father sold our house in Whittier three months after my mother's death and moved to a town house in Newport Beach; he packed up all my books, including *White Gloves and Party Manners,* and there it sat in a box, in the garage, for the next decade.

THE BEST-KEPT SECRET about grief is there are some things from which you never fully recover. Grief is a chronic ailment, like seasonal allergies. Sometimes it's worse than others, some days (her birthday, her deathday, any holiday that requires the producing of a huge ham or prime rib) are worse than others, year in, year out. Grief is not something to be gotten through, like a boring dinner party or an algebra class. We claim to move through it in order to endure it. My mother's death when she was forty-seven and I was eighteen maimed me, has given my life a distinct limp. It was 1975. No one thought I might benefit from grief counseling, or any counseling, for that matter. We Karbos were tough Polacks. My father said so, and since he was the only one I had left, I had no choice but to believe him.

After my mother died, the Mahoneys, even Lorraine and Julia, vanished from our lives. Our connection loosened so easily, it was hard to believe it had ever existed. No more long, ominous evenings, the adults with their cigarettes and their drinks perched upon their knees, Jeri and I inmates sharing a cell in the prison of their entanglement, gone gone gone, never to return. The last Christmas with my mother was the last Christmas with them.

AFTER MY FATHER moved to Newport Beach, and then began dating a woman he'd dated in college, whom he eventually married, they fell off the face of the earth. Or maybe I was the one who fell. When I was a sophomore, a scant eleven months after my mom's death, my father sent me on an expensive study-abroad program, Semester at Sea. Billed as shipboard learning, it was a four-month global circumnavigation departing from Port Everglades, Florida, and returning to Long Beach, California. I turned nineteen in Accra, Ghana. I was happy; for 120 days I pretended to everyone I met — to my fellow students and teachers and the French accountant I met in Abidjan and with whom I had a three-night stand — that my mother was alive and well in southern California, throwing cocktail parties and sending me care packages.

IN THE FIRST house I bought with my first husband, whom I'd met in graduate school, we had a built-in floor-to-ceiling bookcase in our bedroom. This meant that every box of books we'd been dragging around from apartment to apartment could be unloaded. Late one afternoon I opened a box and spied the jewel-toned spines of the all books I'd received for Easter while my mother had been alive. I knew immediately what else I would find; there at the very bottom was *White Gloves and Party Manners*. By then I'd had enough therapy to access my eyeball-popping anger, the adolescent rage that had been unexpectedly short-circuited upon my mother's death.

The book became emblematic of everything I felt angry

about regarding my mother, which was everything, including the fact she had the gall to die, just as I was getting around to telling her I wished she was dead. I left the book out on our rickety Goodwill coffee table, and occasionally read from it as a party trick. I claimed to have thought it was hilarious. "It will tell you what to do and what to say to make people like you." I would read to my friends from the introduction, one time so pissed off a thread of spittle flew from my mouth and landed in the middle of the page. I could have performed it on stage as a piece of political theater.

I had become no one my mother would have recognized. I had not one but two college degrees. I lived with my boyfriends, made my own money, read Kafka, quoted Kafka, refused to learn how to cook, wore steel-toed cowboy boots and drank scotch, neat, worked at being as smart as I could possibly be, was funny not sweet, used *fuck* as an adjective (as in, "that fucking book"). The young woman I had become would have put her in the ground. But, of course, she was already there, so what did it matter?

Then, more years passed, and I had some more therapy, and my own daughter, and I forgave her a little. I was embarrassed at having been so predictable in rebelling. Some of what she taught me made sense. It was good to have manners, and to refrain from parading your intelligence around as if it were a Kentucky Derby winner. Upon my daughter's birth I saw, immediately, that mothers come fully equipped with complete lives that their children couldn't begin to imagine. I came to the conclusion that my mom had been desperate to stay attached to the Mahoneys out of some complicated combination of guilt that she had left her working-class family behind, and one-upsmanship. She'd left them behind, but she wanted them to remember that she had, as often as possible.

But my forgiveness was misplaced; I would learn that I was wrong.

My father died in 2000, of lung cancer. He was seventy-five, having survived both his second wife and fifty years of two packs a day. I wrote a book that won some acclaim about caring for him during his last year of life. On the day he died, after the hospice people came and collected his body, I came upon a safety-deposit box in his closet. Inside there were the usual important documents: the death certificates of my mother and his second wife, Beverly; his two marriage certificates; his and my birth certificates; the legal document indicating that our name was changed from Karbowski to Karbo. At the bottom of the box there was a small, yellowing envelope from the Detroit Legal News Company, dated two years before my parents were married. Inside the envelope there was a two-by-two-inch news clipping, a legal notice stating that the Wayne County Probate Court had approved my mother's petition to change her name from Joan Mary Rex to Joan Mary Sharkey.

I held the square on the palm of my hand. My mother's secret, which my father had dutifully kept until they were both gone. I immediately suspected that my mother had had a previous marriage. Wasn't her beauty legendary? Wasn't she twenty-five (i.e., old) when she married my father, thereby giving her plenty of time for a disastrous first marriage to Mr. Rex? I enlisted a friend, a retired Los Angeles County deputy sheriff turned private investigator, who set the record straight in under an hour. My mother, it turned out, was not a Sharkey. She was not the daughter of Maud, the much younger sister of Lorraine and Julia, the aunt of Mary. According to her birth certificate, she was the daughter of Calvin Rex, age nineteen, and Nora Carrigan, age seventeen. She had not been formally adopted by Maud, but still carried her father's name, Rex, until she became engaged to my father and changed it to Sharkey. She must have wanted the record to reflect that she was not a foster child, not a foundling left at the boardinghouse in Ypsilanti run by Maud Sharkey, the woman I thought was my grandmother.

Aside from a weird sense of relational vertigo, where the people I was told were my people were not my people at all, I was elated. I'd known from the time I was small that there was something off about the way we all interacted. This was it. My intuition was to be trusted after all. I wasn't even eyeball-popping angry that my mother used to explain that the reason I needed to be nice to Jeri was that we were *cousins*. Which we weren't. We were nothing. My mother, the love child of a pair of teenagers with whom we had no connection, had kept us hitched to the Mahoneys not out of guilt, but out of desperation. They were the closest thing to family my mother had, her fake family of origin. But as in all families of origin, fake or otherwise, she had a lot of unfinished business with them. And then she died.

And I was wrong again.

In 2009 I was giving a talk at a gallery in southern California. I'd had trouble finding a place to park and was running late. As I rushed in the door I noticed a young blond woman in an orange sleeveless dress note my arrival and duck into the office at the end of the room. So clearly was she waiting for me, I thought she worked there, and someone had asked her to notify them when I'd arrived.

I came around the corner, into the office, and there was Aunt Mary, whom I hadn't seen in over thirty years. I'd know that blue-eyed glare anywhere. She'd read about my appearance in the newspaper and had come to say her piece. She skittered around the corner, into the main gallery space, and waved in the direction of two blonds—Jeri and her daughter, I guess. Jeri had had some work done. There were teeth and breasts and lots of hair. She looked great. I opened my mouth to tell her so, even though, at the same time, I wanted to go over and ask why the hell, at her age, she was party to this ambush, but Aunt Mary started in.

"I read that book you wrote about us," she said.

"Uh . . . ," I said. What book was she talking about? The

book I'd written about my dad, in which I made passing
mention of the Mahoneys? But there was no time to get my
bearings in the conversation, or to figure out what she was
even talking about. She was there to take me down, and she
was so eager to do it, she didn't give me any time to respond.
I noted, almost without realizing it, that she was overdressed,
in a gold and blue brocaded tunic and skirt, something the
mother of the bride would wear.

"We would have come to scatter your father's ashes, you
know."

"OK," I said.

"You just had to ask!"

"Uh—"

"And Gramma? She's dead."

"Lorraine, you mean? I'm so sorry to—"

"She died five years ago."

"Oh—"

"And Gramma? Gramma was your gramma."

"Gramma was my gramma?" It took me a minute. Lorraine,
my mother's sister, whom I'd been instructed to call Gramma,
even though she was my aunt, was actually my mother's
mother? Is that what she was trying to tell me?

"Gramma *was* your gramma."

I felt as if we were freemasons, or members of some
other secret society that required the exchange of cryptic
passwords.

"OK. Well. It's good to see you. Thanks so much for coming." I leaned down and gave her the most insincere hug ever exchanged between two human beings. If she thought this would rattle me, she was mistaken. I was a Karbo, and one tough Polack. They sat through my talk, then left during the Q & A.

As I WRITE this, I still don't know to whom my mother was born. If Lorraine was really her mother, if Gramma was my gramma, then who was Nora Carrigan, the woman listed on my mother's birth certificate? Lorraine's nom de unwed mother? If so, that would make Aunt Mary not my mother's niece, but her half sister. Perhaps during those long hours spent with the Mahoneys what I was witnessing between them was the secret war between siblings.

Another daughter might want a definitive answer, but I know what I need to know about my mother. For decades now, I've not just supported myself, but also my family, mostly by my wits. Some nights I'd lie awake wondering how I could continue to do this when I'd had no mother to model anything close to the skills I needed to keep going, wishing that I'd had a mother who had at least held a job, who knew how a mortgage refinance worked, or an income-tax audit. I cursed my mother for being a sheltered housewife. Now that I know the truth about her shame, if not about her story, I realize that she, too, traveled up and out into the world in a way that no one, certainly not her unmarried teenaged parents, whomever they may have been, could have possibly expected. I'm sure she also lay awake nights and wondered how to throw a dinner party for my father's boss, or the chair of the board of a volunteer organization she belonged to, when there had been no mother before her to help her through it.

The gift of *White Gloves and Party Manners* was more about my mother than it was ever about me. She'd known from the time she was small that she had to be good, pretty, neat, cheerful, and polite, or be cast aside. The mystery remains a mystery, but I've made peace with it. *White Gloves and Party Manners* sits on a shelf beside my desk, between my French-English dictionary and a copy of Rilke's *Letters to a Young Poet*. Once, years ago, I got a magazine assignment that involved meeting President Clinton. I consulted the book to see how I should address him.

Her Favorite Neutral

· ·

CHARLOTTE SILVER

I once watched my mother put out a fire with her bare hands. She was a chef and her hands, from decades of being in the kitchen, were tough. This happened in the old days when the restaurant she owned in Harvard Square used to have something called Cabaret Night, for which we hosted an old-fashioned supper club in the Club Bar with black-and-white diamond floors and the stuffed crocodiles that Teddy Roosevelt had shot mounted above the fireplace.

On one of those nights, a cabaret singer stood under those stuffed crocodiles belting out a Peggy Lee song called "I Love the Way You're Breaking My Heart." "Although you're gonna ruin it, it's heaven while you're doin' it," she sang, and then, before anyone saw it coming, the sheet music brushed the tip of one of the candles and burst into flames. Back then, you still could use real candles in restaurants; you could smoke indoors, too.

We had not had a serious fire since I was little, when one of the kitchen pipes burst into flames. But because the restaurant, named Upstairs at the Pudding, was located in a drafty old Victorian building, the threat of fire loomed as a perpetual fear.

And so, the night the sheet music ignited, my mother didn't waste a second. She jetted across the black-and-white diamonds to the piano and sliced her hands karate-style through the thickening flames. She did it; she put it out. The show, as they say, went on. The cabaret singer resumed her song, the bartenders rattled their cocktail shakers, customers returned to bowls of vichyssoise on beds of cracked ice.

That night, my mother was wearing a pair of black satin pumps with ribbons that laced ballerina-style up the ankles and, continuing this romantic sketch in a rather Degas mode, a full skirt with crackling layers of bluish violet tulle underneath.

Also, sunglasses: enormous Chanel frames sweeping movie star–style across her face, the lenses tinted a custom shade of lavender.

Also, a cocktail coat: this particular one comes back to me as a cloud of white chiffon.

These, these were my mother's trademarks, her badges of feminine armor against the world.

IT HELPED, OF course, that she was beautiful. In her youth she was said to resemble Kim Novak and even worked, briefly, as a bikini model. And in dreary old Cambridge, Massachusetts, where the Puritan influence reigns in the genteelly faded color palette of the houses and the sensible shoes of the women, my mother is notorious for these sunglasses and for her style of feminine *abbondanza* at large. Pink is her favorite color, though not the wimpy pink of little girls but the lustier, more femme-fatale shades of adulthood. And leopard print her favorite pattern, the motif of a long series of gifts to me, some bought, some new, but many given straight from her closet.

In my mother's universe and later on in mine, leopard was not so much a pattern as a piece of the background. "Leopard," she used to say, "it's my favorite neutral." Plaid was also a neutral, and she enjoyed both plaid and leopard in combination, a preference for theatricality in self-presentation that is another one of her gifts to me.

When I was a child, my mother dressed me in the classics: sailor dresses in summertime, black velveteen ones come Christmas. But when I was in my early twenties and began to ransack her closet for inspiration, it was often the leopard-print items that I reached for and which she, in her usual spirit of generosity, agreed to pass down.

One thing I could not get my hands on, though, was her most beloved piece of clothing, the one which, more than any other, marked her territory: a leopard-print Italian swing coat, lined in mocha velveteen. She bought it in my childhood and wears it still; I just turned thirty.

Of course a leopard-patterned coat is the leopard item to end all others. The year I was twenty-two, my mother gave me a new one for Christmas. It infused the streets of Cambridge with urban glamour and my life with a thrilling sense of toughness it had not previously possessed. I am speaking here of illusions, for Cambridge had no glamour and I, at that stage in my life, no toughness to speak of. But the coat, with its fabulous contrast of honeyed blond faux fur and oyster-sized jet buttons, suggested that both of these things might one day be possible.

The years passed and other hand-me-downs followed — a leopard capelet, the throat of which closed firmly yet sweetly with a black pom-pom; a leopard collar she'd bought in Paris; and a pair of leopard-spotted Ferragamo pumps, spiky, inimitably, even ruthlessly Italian. They were too high for me, those beautiful shoes, those gorgeous things, but I trotted them out on the rare occasions where I considered the danger worth it, and was dazzled, as ever when putting on high heels, by my transformation into a dizzy, imperiled creature: a sensation which is, to me anyway, highly sexual and not at all unpleasant.

It seems to me that animal prints are all about the sensuality and the intoxication of contrast. The brutality, the suggestion of violence of the pattern must be softened, thrown into relief, by the lushness of the fabric, the inviting, touchable nature of it. *Come close,* a leopard collar says to the other observer, *but not too close.* Leopard invites and repels intimacy. In the same instant, it allures and imposes boundaries.

In this way, leopard prints achieve the same function as my mother's sunglasses. They turn heads yet preserve mystery. Not for nothing are animal prints said to be a kind of camouflage.

Camouflage, illusion, indirection, enchantment — my mother was in favor of all of the above. The lighting at the restaurant, and in our home, was pink, care of rose-colored lightbulbs. Paints were high-gloss. Fresh flowers necessary, and one's conversational style encouraged to be charming and evasive. The art of evasion, indeed, was part of the charm.

It was all of a piece; all a kingdom of camouflage, one way or another.

When I was younger, I used to despair of this. When I was younger, I thought this wasn't fair. I thought my mother's policy — this policy of the indirect over the direct, the veiled pink lightbulb over the naked yellow one — wasn't the truth. I thought of it as all some kind of loopy pretense. For I still believed, then, that concepts like fairness and truth could be neatly identified and labeled in any given situation.

I don't believe that now. No, I have come not to believe in such swift certainty of judgment at all. I have come not only to admire my mother's emphasis on personal style, but even to aspire to something like it myself. I have come to see, as

my mother did before me, the unexpected solace of sur-
faces — that they can bear a strong correlation to the state
of one's mental health. As life went on, I often found that
whenever I was in one of my periodic episodes of despair,
I had only to reach into my closet for one of my mother's
hand-me-downs to remind myself that I could sally forth to
face the world after all.

There is a wonderful saying of Oscar Wilde's: "A man's face
is his autobiography. A woman's face is her work of fiction."
This is a comic distinction with which my mother would
have been swift to concur. Her face — skin oiled with Crème
de La Mer, eyes shadowed with gentle, impressionistic swirls
of lavender and almond powder, brows daintily plucked and
blackened — was an elaborate, Wildean, masterpiece.

WHEN, LATER ON in my twenties, I moved to New
York City, my mother mailed me packages from Boston,
glutted with goodies. My roommate and I would exclaim
at the largesse of it all: vintage Missoni dresses; beribboned
Manolo slingbacks in fabrics ranging from python to tweed;
a Ferragamo purse, Bordeaux leather with fat cognac-colored
handles; a Fendi animal-print jacket, palest pink zebra
rather than the more ubiquitous leopard. I wore all of these
gifts, often.

And because they were hand-me-downs, whenever I wore
them it was as though I were wearing my mother's skin. It

is a tribute to just how much I respect my mother that this closeness to her—I can even smell on some of these pieces the haunting residue of her trademark Joy Perfume—filled me not with a prickly discomfort or exasperation but with optimism. I wish I could strut into a room with half of her glory, her panache.

Like all mothers and daughters, we sometimes have our disagreements about my appearance, which is like hers in many ways but unlike it in others. For a long time, she begged me to wear lipstick. "I just think that the more feminine you are," she would say, "the more masculine it makes men feel, and then it all works out . . . for the better." She would trail off and I would be left wondering just what "for the better" in her estimation meant. And for a long time I couldn't reconcile what seemed to me to be a vexing contradiction in this piece of advice, especially coming from my mother, a woman who was wont to tell me, "Remember, Charlotte, relationships are a question, not an answer," and who was not, at any point in her life that I know of, dependent on or under the spell of a man.

And yet it was still essential, according to her code of etiquette, to court the male gaze with lipstick. In fact, several years ago, when Versace discontinued an exquisite shade of violet she'd taken to wearing, a rich and complex tinge with ghostly pink and blue notes surging underneath the slickness of the gloss, she took matters into her own hands and found a company that makes custom shades of lipsticks for a persnickety clientele. When I asked her why she had gone to such lengths, she admitted cheerfully and even, I thought, endearingly, to the simplest of all motivations: vanity.

I am not so vain, myself—I am not so vain at all. I appreciate Beauty but am not, as the expression goes, "high-maintenance." I never have taken to wearing lipstick. I do not care for it, do not feel like myself in it, at all. And while my mother is the type of woman who prefers to saunter in high heels, I am the type who, most days, prefers to speed-walk in ballet flats. So like all daughters, I take some parts of my mother and am free to reject others. I take a love of cinch belts, black lace bodysuits, cocktail coats, and, yes, leopard print, but leave to her stilettos and dramatic maquillage.

"Blonder, blonder, blonder!" is my mother's rallying cry about my appearance. "I'll tell you what, Charlotte. You should get more highlights and have your eyebrows darkened. Have them darkened permanently. You have fabulous eyebrows! The shape of them. But not the color. Go get them darkened and then they'll be gorgeous!"

Blonder, blonder, blonder; darker, darker, darker! These commands are typical of my mother, who adores contrast and tension, tumult and chaos, and who prefers high-gloss paint to matte, big, blowsy flowers to tight, tiny ones.

But recently I decided that it was time not to go blonder but to grow out my highlights after years of getting them done. Perhaps on some deeper, more rebellious level this was an attempt to differentiate myself from my mother, that Kim

Novak look-alike who is so very much a blond. Or perhaps it was just that I wanted a change. Who knows? In any event, the way my natural hair color is growing out—in streaks of moody, deepening ash and gold—rather pleases me. The effect is not so flashy as the baby blond I had affected before, not so eager for attention, rather mysterious, ombre-like: to my mind, a soothing kind of camouflage, in fact.

But what of courting the male gaze, you ask? What of all that? That to me has never, necessarily, been the point of this, or not the main point. I see feminine artifice as a delightful thing for the sake of itself. That I have a mother who is in favor not only of camouflage, illusion, indirection, enchantment but also beauty, sensuality, flirtation, in a word, pleasure—this, too, I have come to look on as a gift. For what is the alternative? To settle to live in a grim, a dingy, a matte-paint world?

THE LAST TIME I went home to Cambridge, my mother presented me with yet another hand-me-down—another gift: a pair of leopard-print Italian ankle boots, rakishly hooded with black velvet at the top. The label, dating to the 1980s, was a name I didn't recognize. The heels, thank God, were a less treacherous height than the Ferragamo spikes I had dared to totter around in on occasion when I was younger, and as soon as I put the boots on I knew that this coming winter would find me wearing them frequently in New York. As I packed them in my suitcase, I understood that this pair of boots, in my mother's "favorite neutral," were just the thing to resolve this contradiction: that with them I might straddle, as my mother did, the line between hard and soft, tigress and enchantress. With them on my feet, I would never feel less than confident.

Only a couple of days after arriving back in New York, I happened to see in the sculpture garden at MoMA an older European woman — I presumed Italian — whose presence captured my imagination. Now that I am in my thirties, I find it is faces like this stranger's that are apt to do this; that I yearn to follow an older face behind a pair of sunglasses more than I do a younger, dewy one without them. This particular stranger had, in addition to sunglasses, slashing black eyebrows, a voluptuously bustled olive-green satin trench coat, and, the perfect touch, on her feet a pair of pointy leopard-print pumps. This woman, who was sultry and dark, couldn't help but remind me of my mother, who of course is still celestially blond. But the effect — the exuberant affirmation of femininity, and the promise of feminine experience — was the same. And something, I thought, to behold. I left the sculpture garden that day with a stirring sense of the winter season to come, and its inevitable events at which I would wear, perhaps with success, my mother's latest hand-me-down, my darling leopard ankle boots.

"I just wasn't capable," she remarked to me once, "of a small life in a minor key."

Someday, I hope to be able to say the same.

Right at My Fingertips

· ·

RITA DOVE

The gifts my mother had given me—over four decades worth—were lost in a house fire on Labor Day 1998. It was the first rainstorm after a parched summer, the first lightning bolt . . . and suddenly the sentimental treasures of my youth, from ribbons and popsicle-stick constructions to old letters and an heirloom brooch, went up, quite literally, in smoke.

I remember standing at the foot of our driveway around midnight watching as the flames leapt, settled back, then flared up again in another spot, leapfrogging from one air pocket to the next. I pictured the progress of the fire inside the house while mentally bidding good-bye to our accumulated lives: our daughter's baby clothes in the attic, the first editions on the hallway bookshelves, tourist T-shirts and prescription pills, my favorite purple bra. As the rooms burst into giant Molotovs, I whispered: "I guess I can live without that."

Remarkable what we can live without. The house was rebuilt and refurnished, new stuff accumulated to fill the shelves and end tables. Gone forever, though, were the little things that sparked memories so keenly—my mother's letters when I was in college, my first pearl necklace, the recipe card I lifted from her flour-dusted index box. (I'd copied the instructions onto a fresh card to replace the one I'd stolen; I wanted to see the recipe in her handwriting whenever I baked the Yeasty Cookies that carried me through my junior year.)

And yet there is one gift from my mother that survived, a display that lies right at hand; every day I look down at them and smile. My fingertips, I mean: ten brilliantly patterned nails, each sporting two colors on the diagonal—gold tips with bottom diagonals of purple, green, turquoise, fuchsia, and coral. Long before "Flo-Jo," the Olympian sprinter Florence Griffith Joyner, I was painting my nails in stripes and polka dots, heraldic fields and fantastical coats of arms—in fact, more than forty years have passed since the spring day when that long-awaited Avon shipment arrived. But I'm getting ahead of myself.

I grew up in a fairly religious community with strict (though mostly unspoken) rules: no talking back to adults, no chewing gum, no makeup before the age of fifteen. This did not mean, however, that we loped about dressed like little girls on the prairie; earrings were encouraged, chic ensembles and snappy shoes de rigueur, especially on Sunday mornings. This schizophrenia reigned in my own family as well: I wore gloves and anklets to church until I turned twelve, when the anklets were jettisoned; from the time I was ten, I could predict my father's birthday presents—a nice piece of jewelry (dangling peridot earrings, an onyx ring) and a briefcase. My grandmother had been a practicing Catholic until her move up North unmasked the latent prejudices of that reputed promised land; barred from Akron's Catholic community, she joined the African Methodist Episcopal Church, where women took the phrase "putting on your Sunday best" to heart. She became a milliner, famed for her elaborate Sunday-go-to-meeting hats.

Fashion was in the genes. Before marrying my father, my mother had worked as a seamstress in a dress shop; she sewed all her own clothes and made sure her daughters greeted sunrise service every Easter in brand-new exquisitely tailored dress-and-coat ensembles fresh from her needle. She wore rouge and lipstick while working around the house and took out her pin curls each morning before coming downstairs to make breakfast. We pored over Butterick patterns together, and I would squeeze onto the couch beside her whenever the Avon lady came calling, with her valise of little flasks and silvery tubes.

One Saturday afternoon found me flipping through the Avon catalog's offerings, dreaming of the day when I would be allowed to sweep dazzling minerals over my eyelids like Cleopatra and enflame my lips like my namesake, Rita Hayworth. Unfortunately, that spring the fashion moguls had called for pastels, and Avon was toeing the line. Even their nail polish adhered to the prescribed color palette, boasting the usual array of frosted pinks. I was disappointed, sad even, until I saw the promotion: FOR A LIMITED TIME ONLY, two quirky new hues, Robin's Egg Blue and Sea Foam Green.

I leapt up to show Mom. Absolutely not, she said. I cajoled, I reasoned, I begged. I was almost fifteen, I wasn't asking for eyeliner, I didn't plan on flaunting red claws like some *Jezebel*! What harm could painting my fingernails do? It might even stop me from biting my cuticles. And the green—that sea foam green would match my Easter outfit *perfectly*. After all, it was nothing more than . . . than . . . finger jewelry!

TO THIS DAY, I think my mother gave in because she figured the polishes were too wacky to stand the test of time. Pastel polish against brown skin was bound to look peculiar; after the first few applications, I would surely lose my nerve. And I almost did. When the order finally came in and I unwrapped the coveted parcel—two sleek bottles, my very own indulgence!—I swallowed hard. As far as blues and greens went, these seemed awfully pale . . . more

Baby Nursery than Femme Fatale. But I knew my manners: I thanked the Avon representative, hugged my mother, then scurried off to my room to explore my options in private.

The first experiments were disastrous: arrayed in Robin's Egg Blue, my right hand looked vaguely frostbitten, while my left hand looked like a tray of after-dinner mints spilled across a mahogany table. But what if I stopped thinking of my nails as natural extensions of my fingers? What if I treated them like ornaments, as boldly artificial as baubles? Since Easter was on its way, why not decorate them like Easter eggs? I tried alternating tints, then used both colors to bisect each nail, adding tiny polka dots in the contrasting shade . . . ah! It was the beginning of a beautiful friendship.

A woman of her word, my mother did not revoke my nail-painting privileges after the Easter eggs had had their day. My request for a contrasting color in order to create borders was granted: a bright pink. Then, in the wake of the Summer of Love, came the psychedelic shades—fuchsia, chartreuse, cobalt, lemon yellow, black. I filled a notepad with designs, each one more elaborate than the last: red and white stripes, orange zigzags, four-color checkerboards. I took care to coordinate my nails with my school clothes each week, while holidays brought out the specialty logos—pumpkins and black cats, green wreaths and snowmen, fireworks against inky skies.

My cuticles grew back, but the decorated nails stayed. "You're so creative, a true artist!" the ladies at church would gush,

and my mother beamed. Gradually, inexorably, my fingernails became both trademark and smoke screen, the badge I
held up to an increasingly inquisitive world—a gambit my
mother, with her rouge and tailored clothes, understood all
too well. When I was a college freshman and found myself
swamped with assignments, I tried going without my multi-
colored polish for a brief time, even no polish at all; but the
sight of my blanched fingertips was so depressing that I soon
returned to my weekly lacquer ritual, patching the tips when
time was short.

Nowadays, my busy schedule demands a speedy
beauty regimen. I'll often scale back the design to a diagonal
divide with a different color on each bottom half and gold
on all the tips, a pattern guaranteed to match nearly any
outfit, simple enough that I can do my nails on the run—in
a car or on a bus, aboard a train as well as a plane—yet still
capable of provoking delight: not everyone has a rainbow at
their fingertips.

So my mother's gift—one she hadn't intended to give—is
a mutable one. Yet it is also very tangible; for every time I
sit down to decorate my nails in the bold designs that have
become my trademark, I think of my mother—who watched
as I crossed the threshold into womanhood and allowed me
to do it my own way.

Midnight Typing

· ·

LUANNE RICE

My favorite gift from my mother is a small pen-and-ink drawing she made on a folded-up piece of typing paper. It depicts
Gelsey, her ragamuffin Scottie, along with the words, in shaky
handwriting, "Beware of wee ferocious beastie." She'd taped
it to the kitchen door of her cottage on the rocks above Long
Island Sound, where she was dying of a brain tumor.

The sign was quintessential Lucille Arrigan Rice. It managed
to be endearing, self-protective, and manipulative all at once.
Translated, it said, "Don't bother me, but if you do, don't let
the dog out, and please think I'm loveable." She hoped being
thought loveable would make up for being thought grotesque.
She had had surgery to debride infected parts of her skull after
removal of the tumor, and her head had collapsed like a rotten
pumpkin.

People showed up at her house every day, especially the visiting nurse, neighbors bearing meals, and the South Lyme ambulance crew, summoned by the push of the Lifeline medical alert button she wore around her neck, if she could get to it in time, before losing consciousness from yet another seizure.

She spent most of her time writing, and too many intrusions kept her from focusing on her novel. As a college student she'd had short stories published in the *Saturday Evening Post* and a play produced in Boston. After graduation, she married my father, a devilishly handsome and tortured Irish Catholic rake, just home from World War II. She must have hoped her early promise as a writer would grow, but then she had three daughters. We spent our lives on pins and needles, wondering if my father would come home each night. Early on I learned to smell his breath for alcohol, and to feel gripped by jealousy for the women he preferred to my mother, my sisters, and me.

My mother had a cheating husband, three little girls, and the burning desire not only to write, but to *be* a writer and have a writing life. We didn't have much money and although I remember worrying, at the age of nine, whether we'd have enough to pay the bills that month, my mother always managed to keep subscriptions to the *New Yorker* and the *Atlantic Monthly*.

Every night, after my sisters and I were in bed, she would

sit at the dining table and write. The sound of her typing would drift upstairs, soft and steady, a lullaby that let me know she was there in a way I never felt when we were face-to-face. The clack of those keys and the bell of the carriage return were code to me. As I lay still, listening, I felt my mother sharing what really mattered to her.

During the day she cleaned the house with Mim, her mother, who lived with us. I'd stay home from school a lot, sometimes half the days of the academic year, not because I was sick, but because I felt the need to stand guard and make sure Nothing Bad Happened—that my father wouldn't die in a drunken crash, or be stolen by someone else's wife, and that my parents wouldn't get divorced.

Spending those missed school days upstairs in the room I shared with both my sisters, I'd hear my mother and Mim talking in hushed tones, my mother emotional and Mim tsk-tsking my father. The smell of floor wax, white vinegar, and Pine-Sol would waft through the air.

Along the way my mother went to night school, got a master's degree in education, and began teaching English at a junior high because we needed the money and health insurance. Her studies and new teaching job distracted her from both writing and motherhood, in just about equal proportions.

My mother didn't talk much to my sisters and me. We called her "the mother figure," intending no irony. During our childhoods, Mim was hands-on maternal, rocking us when we cried, giving us baths in cornstarch when we had the chicken pox, telling us to stop sucking our thumbs unless we wanted buckteeth. As adults we compared notes and realized not one of us remembered our mother ever hugging us.

Mim was the keeper of my mother's flame, knowing she had been cut out for a life more creative and celebrated than the one she had. My mother was burdened by daughters, a wayward husband, and internal conflict. I see her as living in limbo with motherly responsibilities she couldn't quite meet, and writing dreams she could neither fulfill nor allow to die.

Everything changed when we grew up. Our father died, and all three of us left home. Suddenly we were on our own and so was my mother. My sisters and I married within one year of each other, and my mother loved having sons-in-law. She wanted us home every weekend. My then-husband and I would take the train from New York, laden with bags from Balducci's, and we'd cook elaborate dinners, drink wine and Armagnac, talk about books and writing.

For her sixtieth birthday—August 4, 1984—my sisters and I gave her a Scottish terrier puppy. She had just retired from teaching, to devote herself to writing. Mim and Gelsey were her companions in that little house by the Sound. She gardened and wrote, and cooked and wrote, and welcomed us every weekend. As she began to find happiness in her own life, she finally became a good mother.

Six months later, she got a brain tumor. Unable to care for

her mother, who had developed Alzheimer's, she asked for my help in getting Mim into a nursing home. I had just moved to Paris and flew my mother and Gelsey over—my mother's first ever plane ride—to look after them and drive her for chemo at the American Hospital in Neuilly. We'd have to cut through lines of paparazzi because Rock Hudson was there, dying of AIDS, Elizabeth Taylor at his bedside, and my mother was starstruck.

She never wore a wig. We went shopping on Rue du Faubourg Saint-Honoré and Avenue Georges V for scarves from Hermes and Givenchy, and she'd wrap them around her head, then cover them with a blue velvet riding helmet to protect the hole in her caving-in skull, and she'd walk through that crowd of photographers and fans with beautiful dignity.

When she was well enough, we went to London, to see landmarks my father had talked about from his leaves as navigator bombardier in the Eighth Air Force, including a church where he'd been at Mass when it was hit by a buzz bomb, but mostly to make a literary pilgrimage to the houses of Charles Dickens and Dr. Johnson, and to Stratford-upon-Avon.

By then my first novel was out, and I was working on my second. Writing always came first for me; no midnight typing because I'd spent the day cleaning. I had dropped out of college to do it, and even as a young married woman I was a natural recluse. I wouldn't answer the phone or the door.

My mother would read on the sofa in the apartment on Rue

Chambiges, try to talk to me, but I wouldn't even hear her because I was living another life, as the main character in *Crazy in Love*. She observed my writing behavior, but I had no idea it would affect her the way it did.

She loved those days in Paris and London, and she took the memories and sense of herself as a world traveler back to Connecticut, where she resumed work on her novel in a new way. She made the sign, hung it on the door. She started telling the world to go away—I think maybe because she'd seen me do it, and I'd had a novel published, and that's what she wanted for herself.

She had shown me two sides of a writing life—desire and frustration. In return I gave her the example of obsession and almost maniacal discipline. By the time she died, she'd finished the draft of a novel, "Newport Blues," and submitted it to my agent, who made encouraging comments. My mother glowed at the prospect of revising.

She never actually did the revisions. There wasn't time, but also, I think she'd felt such an accomplishment by finishing her first draft, she could die in peace, as a writer.

I framed her drawing of the wee ferocious beastie. It hangs on the kitchen wall, right by the door where she once taped it as a warning to all visitors, in that same beach cottage where she lived and wrote and grew into being a mother, and where our family still gathers. The drawing reminds me of every single thing about her.

Julia's Child

. . . .

ELINOR LIPMAN

There are several things I know by heart, requiring no notes or source material, and they are mostly along gastronomic lines: You add a fistful of dried split green peas and a parsnip to the water that will become your chicken soup; you don't overbeat the milk and eggs lest your custard not set; and when making latkes, always grate the onion before the potatoes so the glop doesn't turn pink.

I don't know what other daughters learned from their mothers, but mine was a purveyor of homely domestic tricks, imparted not with formal lessons but by osmosis, by example at the stove, in conversation as dough was kneaded or liver chopped.

First, what you should know about Julia Lipman: She was single until she was thirty-six, but answered "twenty-three" when her daughters asked how old she was when she married. She gave birth to me, the second child, six weeks before she turned forty-one. My birth certificate lists "mother's age" as thirty-four, and it wasn't a clerical error. She was dainty. She wore housedresses and aprons and never flats. Her bed slippers were mules and her French twist required hairpins. She used Pond's cold cream on her face, Desert Flower lotion on her hands, and didn't like drinking water out of mugs. She loved the Red Sox, and mild-mannered British mysteries—Ngaio Marsh a favorite—in which crimes were solved calmly. She wore Estée Lauder perfume and never the colors red, pink, or purple. She did not drive a car, play tennis or golf, ride a bicycle, or know how to swim, nor did I ever see her pitch, throw, or catch a ball. She was a queen of arts and crafts: a Brownie leader, a Lowell Girls Club fixture for twenty-five years, sewer, knitter, wallpaperer, gardener extraordinaire.

I wanted to be like my father, who was neither dainty nor fussy in any department. He scraped mold off leftovers and burnt crumbs off toast, while saying cheerfully, "Just doing my duty." I once heard him say, "Julia, what saves you is that slight streak of crudity running through you," meaning the occasional off-color remark she'd murmur that made them both laugh. I once found a petal-shaped piece of sapphire-blue glass in her dresser drawer, and asked her what it was. "Oh, it's from an earring I once had. Daddy stepped on it and broke it when we were dating," she told me. They had met in December and married in March, thirty-seven and thirty-nine years old. A stranger had once stopped her on the street, an older man who asked, "Why is it that someone with a complexion as beautiful as yours isn't married?"

I'm sure she said nothing; I'm sure she shrugged and said, "Oh, I don't know."

But my sister and I and our children, given the opportunity from within a time capsule, might have said to the gentleman, "It probably didn't hurt her skin one bit that she had a condiment phobia."

You see, before there were official vegans, before the era of lactose intolerance and sprue, when the description "picky eaters" referred only to toddlers and children, my mother was famously finicky. I don't mean, if someone served her a hamburger with ketchup, she'd scrape it off and eat it close to plain. I mean, if some unfortunate hostess put ketchup on the bun, my mother would push the offending plate away, unable to eat the accompanying potato chips, and ask for nothing else, her appetite ruined. And maybe eat a shirred egg when she got home. It was like our mother had a condition. She refused to taste anything that came from the grocery aisle displaying the vinegary and the savory, the relishes, the mustards, the pickles of any kind; the salad dressings, the barbecue sauces, the Tabascos, the Worcestershires, or the Als. We didn't even own them. If a visiting relative needed some such lubricant or flavor enhancer, he knew not to ask.

Maybe there are worse things. I am no fan of ketchup. I eat my French fries plain, my fried clams without tartar sauce, and my Reubens without Russian dressing. My favorite mustard is the powdered kind, ground from the seed. Ditto my sister.

Now I feel bad, concentrating on her idiosyncrasies. Our mother loved us dearly. Her chicken and fish, her stews, her meat loaves, her lasagna, kugels, and everything else were flavorful in their own, unadulterated way. Spices and herbs were fine. Lemon juice was a dear friend. She could bake like Julia Child, undaunted by recipes calling for yeast or breast of veal. She made a lemon meringue pie that a food stylist would envy. She baked challah, Irish bread, cinnamon rolls, babkas, Christmas stollen for neighbors, and four different kinds of custard (rice, coconut, Grape-Nut, bread). I have these recipes all on index cards, half in her handwriting and half in mine. She sewed us beautiful clothes — prom dresses of pique and velvet, and impossible little miniature outfits for our Ginny dolls.

By her standards, I was not a purist. As an adult, in my own kitchen, I once looked up from my lunch of leftover cooked vegetables, contaminated with vinaigrette, and found her watching me with a puzzled look.

"What?" I asked.

She shook her head sadly. "I never thought a daughter of mine would like to eat her food cold."

To her, her daughters were food adventurers. My sister introduced guacamole to the family. Watching me dribble balsamic vinegar on a backyard tomato, she asked why I'd do that when it was so delicious plain. I countered, "Don't you put salt on yours? It's like that, Ma." I might have bragged once that a squeeze of ketchup added just the right *je ne sais quoi* to my minestrone. And my college roommate's mother-in-law's recipe I make every time an occasion calls for a brisket? Ketchup again. But never when my mother was visiting. I never tricked her. I used some other tomato reduction because a daughter-hostess has to live with herself.

The gift of her prejudices is that almost everything I eat or contemplate eating, or scrape off my roll, reminds me of her. She is there when I eat leftovers cold, dress a tomato, turn dry mustard into paste. Whenever a buffet lunch serves only tuna, egg, chicken and potato salads, I think, *All she could eat here would be a roll and a pat of butter.* I don't like to drink water from a mug unless I have to, and I've never tasted Thousand Island dressing.

Before she died in 1998, I visited her in the nursing home every day. As I was registering her upon admission, I said to the woman behind the desk, "Above all else, she cannot have condiments. Ever. Could you write this down, please: No mustard, no mayonnaise; no salads *made* with mayonnaise; no ketchup, pickles, relish, or piccalilli. No tartar sauce. No Miracle Whip, either. No salad dressing of any kind. Not even on the side."

Perhaps, in her diminished state, they could have tricked her. But, really, compared to what other grown children might be demanding, wasn't mine a small, benign request? The staff always said she was the sweetest person in the whole place. She'd lost her speech, so it was up to me to explain her religion. I had to make sure that this lucky institution observed the rules of Julia, and that no careless aide would let those poisons touch her lips.

Julia Lipman's Salad Dressing
Juice of a fresh lemon; salt, pepper, paprika to taste.

The Deal

. . . .

MARTHA McPHEE

I was being thrown out of an illegal sublet on Claremont and La Salle in Harlem. The apartment belonged to Columbia University, and I was renting it from two professors who'd taken jobs elsewhere but hadn't wanted to let go of a low-rent rental in New York City. Columbia had caught on and I was being evicted. It was 1990, and I'd just been accepted to Columbia's MFA program in fiction, but it didn't come with housing for students who already lived in the city. A sister (I have four) referred me to a Realtor who had a knack for finding spacious, rent-stabilized apartments. Her name was Jan, and she worked with a partner who had just one leg.

Together they seemed to know all the deals to be had on the Upper West Side. But the apartments she showed me were

decidedly not deals — enormously expensive, tiny (no roommate possible), smelling of cat pee and looking onto brick
walls. I was twenty-six years old. I had an entry-level job in
publishing that paid two hundred dollars a week and con-
sumed most of my waking hours, and a nighttime job as
a waitress (to earn extra cash) from which I was about to
be fired because I was too exhausted to be charming. Even
so, I was filled with ambition and dreams of becoming
a writer — but still had nowhere to live, and time was running short.

"It will work out," my mother said to me tirelessly over the
phone. A blind faith is hers, and an imagination that allows
for extreme cleverness; these are her gifts to me. I always believed her. As hard as it can be sometimes, I still do.

After seeing another collection of unlivable apartments,
Jan looked at me as if an idea were igniting. "I have the apartment for you." My eyes lit up. "But you'll never be able to
afford it." My eyes dimmed. "It's huge, sweeping city views,
dining room, living room, two beds, three baths, sixteen
hundred square feet, low rent." We were standing on Broadway at 103rd Street, wilted from the last viewing, car alarms
and sirens and horns, a shuffle of people. "Tell me more," I
said. And she did. The apartment was leased to an eccentric
with long fingers, manicured nails, and wild gray hair, an
aspiring pianist with a baby grand in his foyer. He wanted to
move to Long Island, but he, like the professors, didn't want

to let go of his deal unless he could get something for it. He wanted to sell the lease and was asking fifteen thousand dollars in cash. "It's called a key fee," Jan explained. She had long stringy blond hair with red tints and a lovely, animated smile. She had two sons, a pager in her purse that buzzed away like a gremlin, and she liked to say that she was married to her second Israeli. "Let me know if you want to see it," she said and slipped off into a cab, disappearing down Broadway.

"See it," my mother said when I told her. I'd been doing calculations in my head. The rent was a thousand dollars a month. The tiny places I'd been viewing were the same price and more. If I rented out the second bedroom and the dining room for seven hundred dollars a piece, I could live rent free with income. But how would I come up with the fifteen thousand dollars? "It'll work out," my mother said. "See it."

My mother's name is Pryde Breed Brown, a beautiful woman with golden curls and a gap between her teeth. She's the daughter of a Montana cowgirl who had social ambitions that led her to the East and into a marriage with a blue-blooded Bostonian, Charles Mitchell Brown, heir to the Buster Brown shoe factory (which was all but defunct by the time they met) and Breed's pasture on which the Battle of Bunker Hill was fought. When my grandmother set her mind to something, she got it. She could handle any horse, bareback; she could kill a rattlesnake with just one shot; she could catch trout on the end of a willow switch. She chose the name Pryde to honor a girl from childhood who'd been kicked in the head by a horse and killed. She'd raised Pryde to be a lady, dressing her like a doll, sending her to Sweet Briar, a girl's college in the South, seeing she married a Princeton man within a year of graduation. She longed for Pryde to have the conventional life that she had had to fight for. So my mother had four babies all within two years of each other, a big white house in the woods, nothing to do all day but arrange our lives, sew us matching dresses from Liberty of London fabric, and dream up writing assignments my father, a writer, could pursue that would involve long trips with us, his family, to Europe.

"Dream," my mother often said to her daughters. "Whatever you set your mind to you can accomplish."

When, at thirty-two, my mother found herself alone with four young children, and very little knowledge of how to negotiate the world, she took to her bed and didn't get out for several months. That's how it felt to me as a four-year-old. My sisters and I took care of her. We brought her breakfast, creamed chipped beef that we made ourselves at the kitchen stove. We got ourselves ready for school, onto the school bus, home from school. My oldest sister made sure we did our homework each night. My mother had never written a check. She had never paid a bill. She had hardly shopped for clothes for herself. My grandmother was disappointed in her for losing her husband, for allowing the life she wanted my mother to live to shatter.

"It will work out," she told me so many times.

After awhile my mother asked herself what she could do, what she wanted. She got out of bed and changed her life quite completely. She met my stepfather, a poker-playing Texan who drove a turquoise Cadillac. He was a feminist, organizing sit-ins in pubs that excluded women — anything but conventional. He wore ascots and a cowboy hat, had a Texas drawl. She joined a group called Women on Words and Images that was taking apart children's readers, to point out their inherent sexism. With the group, she wrote a book: *Dick and Jane as Victims: Sex Stereotyping in Children's Readers.* She bought a portrait photography business because she recognized that she was good at taking pictures, and started a business which, some forty years later, still thrives in her town of Princeton, New Jersey. She remade herself. She had a fifth daughter. My stepfather was a househusband.

The apartment on the Upper West Side was in a building that was being held by a receiver. That meant it had no actual owner because the previous owner had gone bankrupt in the savings and loan fiascos of the 1980s. The city assigned a company to take care of the building until a purchaser could be found. That meant no one was in charge and no one cared, which translated to opportunities for shady deals.

June of 1990 filled in with gorgeous warm days. Jan took me up to the sixteenth floor, and there to greet us was the pianist with his manicured nails. He carefully showed me around the apartment, which was four times the size of the biggest places I'd seen, with sweeping views, just as Jan had promised: the Chrysler Building, the Pan Am Building, the Empire State and a glimpse of the Trade Towers. Six southern exposure windows overlooked the sea of Manhattan, spires and skyscrapers and water towers — a dream. The kitchen led to a formal dining room to a sprawling living room, and light was everywhere. The master bedroom had an en suite bath and floor-to-ceiling mirrors directly across from the king-size bed.

The pianist patted the bed and told me to sit down: "I only do business on my bed." I sat down. The deal involved the fifteen thousand in cash in exchange for the lease. The lease would be drafted by a lawyer and given to me as soon as I handed over the money. He told me that I wouldn't really be buying the lease: "That would be illegal, of course." Rather, I'd be buying a floor lamp, a chandelier, and a dishwasher. The 1980s burst with such deals, the downside of rent stabilization laws. But by 1990, they were drying up and cash in paper bags for a lease was a rarity that involved even more risk than it had a few years before. But to stumble into such a "deal" was a stroke of good fortune . . . or so I was told by Jan. Of course, there were plenty of stories about being swindled. Only a fool would agree to such a ploy. "How do I know I'll get the lease?" I asked the pianist and then later, Jan. "Don't worry," was all they said. It was one of those times where you just had to trust. I wanted this and needed this so much that I was willing to take the leap, willing to believe. And the possibility of the deal made my blood hot, made me hungry and curious. Somewhere, somehow I was sure it would work out. But still I didn't have the cash.

"Is it really great?" my mother asked over the phone. I described it for her, detailed my plan of living rent free with income, and even imagined that I could use student loans to pay back the fifteen grand, if only I could borrow it from somewhere. My father was not a risk taker of this sort, but my mother, who was, didn't have that kind of money. Yet I could almost hear her scheming on the other end of the line. "I have an idea," she finally said.

Her idea was a man named Barry. A wealthy and bearishly handsome man who wore a diamond pinky ring and a floor-length white fur coat. He owed my mother a favor. He'd been accused of being a peeping tom, of spying on a woman as she undressed, from the window of his home into the window of hers. He hired my mother to take photos that would prove the angle of the windows made it impossible for him to see into his accuser's home. The pictures settled the case in Barry's favor. My mother has a way with people. They fall in love with her. Young, old, it doesn't matter. They are inspired by her charm and her ability to make the impossible seem like the most natural thing in the world.

She arranged for lunch with Barry at the Peacock Inn in

Princeton. It was summer so he didn't wear his coat, but the ring glistened on his pinky. He listened to me intently, a negotiator parsing a transaction, as I spelled out what I needed and why. Hearing myself tell the story to a stranger gave me a start—it seemed more than a little crazy. But my mother, seated across from me, nodded and smiled through it all, as if fifteen grand in a paper bag for a lease was nothing unusual. I explained to Barry that I had a grant from Columbia so I wouldn't need student loans, but that I would take them anyway and pay him back within a year. He heard me out, advised me against what I proposed to do, but gave me the money anyway—a check that I would cash. One hundred and fifty hundred-dollar bills—newly minted, crisp, and filled with possibility. I gave Barry my word: no matter what, I would pay him back within a year.

I was warned by a lot of people. My sisters said it was foolish. I didn't dare tell my father. My best friend told me that it wouldn't amortize, even if it did work out, because I'd fall in love with a rich man and end up on Park Avenue. But I went forward, cash in a paper bag handed over to the long slender fingers of the pianist, a twenty-four-hour wait in which I did not sleep, fearing homelessness and ruin, fancying where, in that huge space, I'd put my desk, feeling at once foolish and clever and eager and the high of the high roller—that gorgeous, terrifying rush of adrenaline.

HERE I SIT, twenty-one years later. My desk overlooks the city. I have watched the Pan Am Building become the MetLife Building. I saw the Twin Towers go down and the plume of smoke slowly turn with the winds and drift north. I saw the Time Warner Center rise, and I watch the Empire State Building change the color of its lights like a woman changing her dress. I never met a man who would take me to Park Avenue. I met a poet instead. We have two children and have written some ten books between us. Here in this apartment, the rent still low, we have been able to live our dream, to be artists and parents, because my mother taught me to take the impossible in stride.

The Plant Whisperer

....

DAHLIA LITHWICK

I was raised in a greenhouse.

My mother, born of Iraqi Jews who had migrated to India, married a Canadian who brought her home to a glass house in Ottawa. As a toddler, I barely noticed that most of the house was made of windows, but it wasn't me paying the heating bills. What I did notice was that every window was always and forever mounded with plants. Delicate African violets and cactuses bloomed, and avocado trees stood sentry over the living room. They must all have been as baffled by the endless Canadian winters as my mother. But more pressing in my memory, we were running a plant infirmary at my house, in which root tipping, stem reinforcing, and plant healing happened in tiny glass jars and chipped mugs on every windowsill.

It was as if my brothers and I had a whole host of plant half siblings guiding us through our childhoods, hopping along on their little plant wheelchairs and slings and crutches.

Of course when I started college, I bought plants for my dorm rooms, and I even have a vague, blurred memory of my mother once walking me through a root transplant over the phone, in the manner of Hawkeye Pierce on *M*A*S*H* talking some rookie surgeon through an amputation by walkie-talkie. When my parents finally moved to the desert, my mother's green world exploded into the outdoors. Suddenly there was jasmine, and hibiscus, and lemon trees so fat with fruit the neighbors would come by with shopping bags. Plants outside the house! If I call her and the phone rings and rings, it just means my mom is out in her garden, snapping off dried leaves and picking out tiny weeds and doing something with something that will someday bloom into something extraordinary.

But then came the plant she gave me when my first son was being born. A painful and violent labor turned into a painful and violent delivery and then got worse. It was going so badly that when my parents left the hospital the first night, my mother tore the printed message off the top of the little card they'd stuck in the plant at the hospital gift shop, which had read WELCOME NEW BABY or some such. A joyous welcome was no longer certain. A few hours later, soon after

Coby emerged, I saw a new, flowering plant by my bed and only the torn bottom half of a card.

I TOOK OUT the worst of my postpartum derangement syndrome on that poor plant. I couldn't help but wonder how my mother imagined I could take care of a tiny white flowering plant over and above the colicky, deranged, sleepless bucket of hair that came out of me crying and couldn't stop for three and a half months (but who's counting?). I wanted to drown that plant. Taking care of it was too much to ask of me.

My son did stop crying, but only after my mother sat up rocking him all night long, so my husband and I could sleep for a few hours and not phone the divorce attorneys. Eight and a half years later, the plant still blooms in an upstairs dormer window. I forget to water it and it lives, I overwater it and it coughs up a lung and then thrives again. Tiny white flowers greet me almost every morning, despite my best efforts to forget it. I once dragged my mother over to the plant and demanded that she explain why it looked so droopy in places.

"Yes, they do that," she said.

Even with its perilous beginnings, that plant is the most precious thing my mother has ever given me. Most of what I know about parenting and patience and life I've learned by watching it. Of my kids, I now mostly think, "Yes, they do that." At some point, I asked my mother what this type of plant is called, and

she said, "It's a Grandma Rose plant," because my grandmother, her mother-in-law, had loved them so much. When
my son turned three, he planted strawberries all over the
backyard garden, and they produce similar tiny white flowers
that—I secretly hope, every spring—might just grow into
my Grandma Rose.

My second son, Sopher, was born without a plant entou-
rage, but with a green thumb in his mouth. He started pop-
ping seeds into the garden as soon as he could toddle, and
the row dedicated to peas is still labeled "pesa" because he
was four and couldn't spell, and really, shouldn't they have
been called pesa in the first place? Last summer, when he was
five, Sopher and I ended up in Home Depot or Lowe's or one
of those huge wretched "home improvement" stores with no
windows anywhere, and he circled four times around a rack
of broken, dead, and diseased plants generously described by
a sign as "lonely plants" but largely marked by their crypt-
like odor. He begged for one. We now have three. He waters
them and names them and tells me he is the "plant whis-
perer," just like his grandmother.

His sunflower grew so big it finally fell over. His tomatoes
are still glorious. Even the pesa. I worry that the neighbors
will come with shopping bags for the pesa. I watch him out
there in wonder.

Voltaire famously concluded *Candide* with the advice,
"But let us cultivate our garden." He understood that there is

something about caring for the plant world that makes us more apt to behave well in the human world. One has the notion that things raised in hothouses come out delicate and fragile. But I think the opposite is true: I think they are raised with an understanding of how life runs deep and sure and all around.

WE CONSIDER OURSELVES a green family. Prius, check. Compost heap, check. But I don't shiver in anticipation at the thought of splitting tubers or transplanting peonies, as my mother does. She reminds me what it is to be of the earth and to fight for the earth, not by way of bumper stickers and committee meetings and petitions, but by just planting and tending and weeding and never giving up on even a broken bit of spider plant. I see that in my son now, too — happy with dirt in his green rubber boots and a watering can and a watermelon seed. When I go to visit my parents, my first stop is my mother's garden. When his lonely plant goes yellow at the edges, my son asks to put in a call to his grandparents. The earth and the garden have rooted us all to one another when nobody was looking. We cultivate our garden and let life take it from there.

Wait Till You See
What I Found for You

∙∙∙

MAMEVE MEDWED

My mother gave me many gifts: her love of humor, peanut butter cups, Dorothy Parker, *New Yorker* cartoons, Cole Porter,
flea markets, libraries, steamed lobsters, raw peas fresh out of
the pod, and silver candlesticks. And even though my father's
twelve-year illness forced her into pinching pennies, she rel-
ished the rare grand gesture — the Waldo Pierce painting, a
restaurant filet mignon (the right side of the menu be damned),
the fur-collared coat she bought me for my twenty-first birthday. Every treat teetered on the seesaw between need and indulgence; as a result, she refused to buy a new refrigerator,
thus requiring the repairman to pay so many service calls we
began to claim him as a relative. And forget any dryer to ac-
company the washer that shook our floors with hurricane-gale

force the minute it segued into spin. Condemned to the backyard clothesline, our sheets froze into rectangles fringed with icicles. She also nixed pajama-party-compulsory Lanz nightgowns and toasty boots for the mile and a half walk to school. Deprivation built character; surprising extras provoked cartwheels of ecstasy in my younger sister and me.

While I can appreciate someone else's large white room filled with light and not much else, I am my mother's daughter when it comes to spurning plain walls and empty tabletops. I support my daughter-in-law's rule of eliminating an old coffee mug for every new one, but my mother's all-addition/no-subtraction approach better suits my kind of math. She collected objects, paintings, furniture until the day she died, convinced there was a place for one more thing in the eight small rooms she inhabited for over sixty years. She always managed to carve out a few more feet for yet another portrait, rearranging the wall's jigsaw to accommodate the latest faux ancestor. Even in her final months, connected to oxygen tanks, she insisted we cart Chippendale chairs and silver trays to her nursing home to recreate a mirror image of a familiar interior.

When we were first married, my husband and I occupied furnished student digs amid a hodgepodge of battered tables and old socks balled into corners by the previous tenants. After graduating, we rented an apartment barely big enough for our desks and books. As a housewarming gift, my mother gave us a four-poster mahogany bed whose finials grazed the low ceilings. We were ecstatic over such a luxury. Measured against restless nights on the fold-down, spine-stabbing, ridged sofa that our friend Louise left us when she moved to Los Angeles, this standard-sized mattress seemed as vast and infinite as the sea.

In 1971, we bought our current house in Cambridge, Massachusetts, thus providing my mother with the best outlet for all her gracious-living dreams. Though it's an 1865 Victorian on a lovely hill, her first reaction crushed us. "But it doesn't have two full baths," she said. (She didn't have two full baths.) "There are a lot of stairs," she said. (She had a lot of stairs.) "No fireplace," she said. (She had no fireplace.) "The kitchen is kind of small," she said. (Hers was smaller). "Why so few closets?" she asked. (Her whole house sported only two phone-booth-sized closets with space, perhaps, for a single Clark Kent Superman cape.)

"Look at the good bones," I said. I pointed out intricate molding and high ceilings. "And as soon as we can afford it, we'll hire an architect and renovate."

"Renovate?" she asked, her lips pursed as if she'd swallowed something sour. *Renovate* was not a word in her vocabulary. Nothing had been renovated in her house for sixty years except for the emergency replacement of the living room wallpaper when it started coming off in sheets so massive even the chockablock paintings couldn't hold back gravity.

"I suppose you could improve it," she allowed, and went on

to describe the house of her best friend's son, Ethan. He'd built it overlooking the ocean, she said. It was gigantic. It had its own beach. The dining table sat fifteen. The kitchen rivaled the Brighton Pavilion's palm tree fantasy. At the end of the bed, in the master bedroom, a movie screen popped up the minute you tapped your foot.

"I would hate that," I protested.

"Of course you would, dear," she sighed. "It's just so grand."

I knew what she wanted for me. Something grand. Gracious living times two. A House Beautiful house. A stately home. Bragging rights.

To please her, I needed only to acquire for myself what she had always coveted for her own self. My mother's happiness was on my shoulders. I had inherited her more-is-more gene while my sister ate off a white plastic table and refused all my mother's home-improvement gifts. "I don't care about fixing up my apartment," my sister said. "I'm never there anyway." My sister had a real job, an office to go to, while I, a writer, worked from my own turf, face-to-face, on an hourly basis, with all my house's inadequacies.

But if my sister didn't care, I cared. And my mother knew it. Besides, my husband and I loved her taste. She could do the heavy lifting, have fun, and also take the burden off us. Let me add that at the time we bought our house, my mother had been widowed for eleven years, taught nursery school, and weighed a no-weakling ninety pounds. So petite was she that antique dealers sold her baby bracelets cheap because nobody else, including well-nourished infants, could clasp them around modern wrists. She wore them by the dozens, clanging when she walked.

Bracelets still clanging, she got to work. With the help of a neighbor, she roped to the top of her rusty Dodge Dart rugs and chairs and tables and, once, a ballroom's gold-leafed mirror bought at an estate sale from a Bar Harbor "cottage" and made the four-and-a-half-hour trip from Bangor to Cambridge. None of her treasures was perfect — the rugs had holes and faded colors, the mirror had lost a whole corner of curlicues, the chair legs were spindly, fit only to hold someone the size of my mother. We accepted all gifts gladly, moving them around our fast filling-up rooms until, at last, my mother declared our house, if not grand, then "interesting." Thrilling us, she added the ultimate compliment: "Even more interesting than Ethan's house." She lowered her voice. "However tiny in comparison."

Though such praise was a real gift, the best was yet to come. "Wait till you see what I found for you," she called one afternoon. Glee marked each syllable. "I'll drive it to Cambridge this weekend, as soon as I can get my neighbor to tie it to the roof."

"Great," we said. "What could it be?" we asked each other.

Three days later, she arrived. We studied the huge, mysterious, tarp-covered bulk lashed to the top of the car with what looked like dangerously flimsy rope. "Bigger than a bread box," my husband quipped.

My mother seemed a little shaky when she stepped onto the sidewalk. "Sea legs," she explained. "It acted like a sail. I was all over the road."

We cut the rope. We pulled off the tarp.

"Ta da!" my mother beamed. Triumphantly, she thrust her braceleted fist into the air.

We grinned. We clapped. "Wow," we chorused and beheld our new front door.

IN THE DECADES before we bought it, our house had gone through multiple renovations — first single family, then two family, followed by a third apartment built into the basement. After so many past lives, the original central entrance had now been switched to the side; its door was flat, nondescript, utilitarian, probably plywood. We varnished it and were satisfied.

But not my mother. Rescued from a wrecking ball, her salvaged treasure had once served as the proud portal to a nineteenth-century Bulfinch house with impressive architectural lineage. The house was in the process of being demolished to make way for a drive-through Chinese restaurant when my mother jumped from her car yelling, "Stop!"

"I got there just in time," she explained.

"Lucky for us," my husband said.

We *were* lucky. This door was a work of art, big, substantial, paneled with intricate raised molding; a large oval brass knob jutted out from a gleaming flower-etched brass plate. "To think it might have ended up in some landfill," my mother groaned. We called my cousin Stevie, an engineering student at MIT and thus qualified as "handy." He widened the frame; he adjusted the threshold. A locksmith came that afternoon to fix the locks and make us keys.

OVER THE LAST forty years, the door has greeted an endless parade of family and friends. An ongoing cycle of tacked-up notes, Post-its, and political leaflets has bannered its panels; truckloads of mail have slid through its slot; bouquets of flowers, fruit baskets, and packages have leaned against its jamb. Our tiny, blanket-swathed newborns, whom we first carried, terrified and exultant, through this door, now have children of their own. Yet again, a new wave of toddlers' hands reaches for the knocker, twists the knob. "We're here. Let us in," they call. Such continuity delights and comforts us.

Though the door has been painted black, crimson, French blue, and is currently park-bench green, its magnificent molding highlighted in Chinese red, these are only superficial changes for what remains our cornerstone. Sometimes I worry about its future. "Can we sell the house without the door?" I ask my husband. Its plywood predecessor is still stored in the basement. "Can we give it to the kids?" One son lives in an apartment; the other prefers spare and modern. "It belongs here," my husband and I conclude.

"Beautiful," pronounced my mother, who used to carry around a photograph of the door along with snapshots of her grandchildren. I picture generations of boys and girls skipping through that door to play in the front yard. I imagine future hands inserting the key, turning the knob, smoothing it, leaving fingerprints. If the eyes are the mirror of the soul, our door is the mirror of the heart of our house. *Welcome,* it says. My mother's gift opens, like the first of Russian nesting dolls, into the gifts beyond that door: the things of hers I have, tangible and intangible. And I know she lives on in the thick, solid, enduring fact of her gift, once set like a sail on top of her car.

Truths in a Ring

· ·

SUSAN STAMBERG

"Oedipus, schmedipus," the old joke went. "As long as you love your mother."

And I did. As did my father. But did he love her more than he loved me? I was much too young, when he gave her that ring, to understand that there were different kinds of love, different kinds of loving. I was an only child, adored and pampered. When he handed her a small package for her birthday, I thrust out my five-year-old hand and grabbed it.

"Oh, no, darling. That's not for you. It's for Mommy."

"Yes, sweetheart. Today is my birthday. Daddy's giving me a present."

What?! This was impossible. Every brightly wrapped and ribboned box I'd ever seen had been for me. And not this one?!

With her lilting, lovely voice (which taught me so much, and read me so many books, and drilled me, years later—again with such attentive love—on boring French verb endings) she was carefully giving me an early, difficult lesson in relationships and possession and consideration. These lessons always were her greatest gifts to her only daughter.

But on that September 3, 1943, when my father handed the pretty box to her, I bawled. Bawled more. And more. Enough so that she took me on her lap and cuddled me while she opened her present. It was a massive pale purple amethyst ring. A rock, really. She loved it, and wore it for special occasions all her life. The last time was at her ninety-fifth birthday party, at the nursing home in Washington, D.C.

She'd moved to Washington from her beloved Manhattan, at our urging, when she was sixty-eight years old. Her large family had scattered. Friends were dying or moving away.

"Come watch your grandson grow up," I said. And she did. She became a fixture in our lives. For thirty years, her presence helped to square off our small triangle of a nuclear family. We Stambergs were three only children under the same roof. Not the easiest combination. My husband, Lou, had Mom's sweetness, but also the determination to excel that propels many only children. Our son, Josh, was strong-willed pretty much from birth. And I, of course, was totally pampered and adored, thanks to those loving parents.

Triangles are always tricky, and while we three Stambergs worked and played well with others, we certainly had our tensions, our juggling for attention. When my mother moved into an apartment building ("just a seven-minute bus ride away," as she frequently pointed out), her presence helped smooth out a number of squabbles. And, eternally tactful, she knew when not to interfere or opine. That's one gift I wish she had given to me!

When I turned sixty-eight, I thought back to what it must have been like for her to have changed her life so radically at that age. The very thought exhausted me—the notion of breaking so many connections built up over a lifetime, and moving to a new place. But she did it with conviction and good humor, because family meant everything to her.

Mom was the youngest in a family of *eight*. A cosseted, adored, beloved little girl, she grew up in Washington Heights—her father (she would proudly tell) was *the* leading designer of women's coats and suits in Manhattan. Fashion was always important to her. She had beautiful, wonderfully made clothes and looked terrific in them—slim and nicely groomed. White gloves always in summer (even for backyard barbecues in Washington). Black leather gloves in winter. And for special occasions, that amethyst ring from Dad was always a perfect adornment.

We were so different, my mother and I. She with all those brothers and sisters. Me, the only child. She learned sweetness and getting along, from those many sibs. I learned contrariness, and how to get away with it. So, because fashion meant so much to her, I wore what we then called dungarees, growing up in the '50s. I always had a weight issue, and was rarely "groomed." Little of that has changed for me. Although, over the years, I've come to look more and more like her. Sometimes, glimpsing a mirror, the resemblance is startling. And gives me deep pleasure, because it's an evolving way I can keep her with me.

TOWARD THE END, she became snappish at times — a tone came into that lilting, beautiful voice that I'd not heard before. She was old and achy, and it made her impatient. I now understand how age can do that to you. I snap, too, from time to time.

But I remember Mom's snappishness, because it was in such contrast to her basic nature.

She was, quite simply, a lovely and lov*ing* woman. That was the gift of her life, and her gift to everyone who met her. She greeted you with shining eyes, a tilt of her head, and a wide smile. She caught your face in her hands, to *really* look at you. And put a world of caring into a simple kiss on the cheek.

She loved to talk, and walk, and visit. She loved music (her voice was full of music when she spoke). And she *sang* wonderfully — harmonized when I played the piano and friends stood around singing the great old songs every Thanksgiving. Music was another gift from her. I visited the nursing home one afternoon and found her and the other third-floor ladies sitting together watching a Nelson Eddy–Jeanette MacDonald movie on the big TV. Mom was singing along with them—just as she had with Judy Garland and *Easter Parade,* the week before.

I sang to her as she died. It was a song she had taught me. I just discovered, from the baby book she kept, that it was the very first song I learned. I love the words, because they're emblematic of *her*—her light grace, her lovely ways. The name of the song is "Alice Blue Gown"—from the 1919 show *Irene* (Mom was thirteen when it opened on Broadway). The lyrics are by Joseph McCarthy (not the witch hunter of Communists; this one could rhyme!). Harry Tierney wrote the music. And Alice blue was the color named for Alice Roosevelt—President Theodore's daughter.

In my sweet little Alice blue gown,
When I first wandered down into town,
I was both proud and shy,
As I felt every eye,
But in every shop window
I'd primp, passing by;
Then in manner of fashion, I'd frown.
And the world seemed to smile all around,
Till it wilted I wore it, I'll always adore it,
My sweet little Alice blue gown.

Anne Rosalind Rosenberg Levitt died in 2003, three months short of her ninety-seventh birthday. Going through her things—papers, clothes, jewelry, all the stuff of life—I came across the amethyst ring in the bottom of her jewelry box. Mom had had some simple diamond jewelry, which I've passed along to my daughter-in-law. And her pretty but not very expensive costume things I distributed to family and friends. But the amethyst ring rests in my bureau drawer. I've never worn it—it's not my style at all—but it sits there like an old story, a lesson in the loves (and losses) of life. And most important, the ring is a reminder of the major things she gave me: kindness, attention, affection, a lifetime of love.

Quilts

. . . .

JOYCE CAROL OATES

My favorite is always on my bed. Even in warm weather.

It is not a large quilt but very beautiful, I think: comprised of numerous brightly colored knitted-wool squares of every imaginable color—red, yellow, green, blue, purple, magenta, brown, cream.

The pattern is neither simple nor complex. It isn't, like some quilts, a labyrinthine design.

From the start, I loved this quilt. Just to look at it is to feel comforted.

Several generations of cats have slept on this quilt. (Even as I write this, my little gray cat Cherie is probably sleeping on it, asprawl in a patch of sunshine.) I can only estimate how many years have passed since my mother gave the quilt to me and my husband Ray Smith: Thirty years? Thirty-five?

The cherished little quilt in all the colors of the rainbow has followed me from one residence to another — in different bedrooms in different houses in different phases of my life.

In this most recent phase, in which the bright-colored quilt is laid on a pale blue comforter on my bed in a house in Princeton, New Jersey, into which I moved in 2009 with my second husband, Charlie Gross, my mother has been absent from my life for nine years.

Nine years! That seems so long, yet my memory of Mom is so vivid, I can glance up and see her in the doorway of my study — I can see the expression on her face, and (almost) hear what she is saying.

My mother never visited this house. She would love it, I think — especially the large curving flower beds, so like the flower beds she'd tended in our yard in Millersport, New York, years ago. When she'd visited Ray and me in my former Princeton home, less than five minutes from this house, Mom had always helped out in the garden, as in the house; we would garden together and prepare meals, while my father, a gifted amateur pianist/organist, played piano in the living room.

Whenever my parents came to visit us in Princeton, my mother would bring gifts for us: mostly items she had knitted, crocheted, or sewn. We have several lovely afghans, including one that is entirely white, with a subtle, delicate design, and another, large and heavy as a comforter, that's made of orange, brown, and white wool. She'd knitted me several sweater-coats, one of them in a vivid crimson wool; she'd sewn the most exquisite blouses—a white long-sleeved blouse in raw silk, which I used to wear often; a pumpkin-colored silk blouse; a dove-gray silk blouse with a fine-stitched collar. For years I wore these blouses, and dresses and jackets my mother had sewn; in many of my "author photos" I'm wearing Mom's clothes. Those I no longer wear are enshrined in my closets—I look at them often, marveling at the fine stitching and hemming, the exquisite small touches, mother-of-pearl buttons, pleated bodices. Dresses, skirts, vests, shawls. Often I wear the shirts she'd sewn for me—white, pink, red, magenta; one of my favorite sweaters is a pink sweater-coat with a knitted belt.

There is nothing so *comforting* as wearing clothes your mother has sewn or knitted for you.

After my mother died in 2003, for a long time I would imagine her with me, in my study in particular, though *imagine* is perhaps a weak word to describe how keenly I felt Mom's presence. In writing the novel *Missing Mom,* I tried to evoke Carolina Oates—well, I'm sure that I did evoke her, not fully or completely but in part. Mom is so much a part of myself, writing the novel was the antithesis of an exorcism, a portrait in words of a remarkable person whom everyone loved.

In February 2008, when Ray was hospitalized, and after he died unexpectedly a week later, I often lay in bed too exhausted to move, beneath the rainbow-colored quilt. The bed became my haven, my refuge, my sanctuary, my nest—with my mother's quilt as a sign of how love endures in the most elemental and comforting of ways. Warmth, beauty, something to *touch*.

In extremis we care very little for the public life—the life of the career—even the life of literature: it is comfort for which we yearn, but comfort can come to us from only a few, intimate sources. I know that I have been very fortunate. I never cease giving thanks for my wonderful parents, who bequeathed me their love and their hope, and for this quilt on my bed, as singular and beautiful in 2012 as it was in the late 1970s.

Finding the Love Child

SHEILA KOHLER

My mother gave me many gifts. She was the sort of generous woman who would, if you admired a diamond ring or a fur coat, take it off and give it to you. Yet at her death in Johannesburg, at seventy-two, she did not leave to me, her only remaining child, the large fortune my father had left her. She had always said to me and my older sister, "Everything I have in the world is yours," though toward the end of her life she had hinted that the money might go elsewhere: "I will have to take care of my own family," she would say mysteriously. I wasn't quite sure what she meant and didn't dare ask.

A few years before her death, staying in her house on a visit from my home in the United States, I rose sleepless one night. I wandered barefoot through the vast, moonlit rooms, with all their heavy Victorian furniture. On a whim, I opened up the drop-leaf desk in what we called the lounge and found her will. I turned on a lamp and read it. She planned to leave much of her fortune to her brother and sisters. What remained was going to a man whom I didn't know. To me, she was leaving her jewelry, her furniture, and a Chinese figurine of a small Buddha. As I sat there in the moonlight, the whole room, with its familiar pink, chintz-covered sofa and armchairs, the drop-leaf desk, the thick, plum-colored wall-to-wall carpet, seemed suddenly strange, as though I had never seen it before. I was no longer, I realized with a dull ache, a much-beloved child, a privileged part of my mother's family, but in some way already an outcast.

By the time of her death, when I was in my early forties, I still didn't know who the mystery heir was, but I took the hurtful will for granted, particularly as my father had left a small part of his fortune directly to my sister and me. Yet when I told people about this, they were always most shocked and puzzled. They asked why she would have done such a thing. And when I was not able to answer that, they asked to whom she left her money.

It was partly this extreme reaction that made me think the story of the will might be a good subject for a novel, one I eventually wrote, after I had gleaned additional and surprising information about my mother's life, which I shall recount, as Dostoyevsky says, in its proper place.

Initially, once I had mentioned the money she left her siblings, there was nothing else I could say. There was so little I knew about my mother. We had spent so little time with her. As little girls we were brought up by an English nanny in a large house and garden. We slept in a nursery and were cared for by the nanny once for eighteen months when our parents went abroad on business. It was on their return that my father had a heart attack and died. Later, we had asked to be sent to boarding school, as most of the girls in our school were boarders, and our mother, though reluctant, obliged us. When I had finished high school, I left South Africa at just seventeen.

I left for many reasons, some of them political; I was afraid that if I stayed I would be forced to protest and have to go to jail. But perhaps the most important reason was that I felt I needed to get away to find out who I was. Not knowing my mother well made it perhaps more difficult to find myself. For many decades, living, studying, and writing, first in France and then America, I explored this question of identity in three collections of short stories and seven novels. Some of these were historical, based on the lives of brave women, like the Brontë sisters, or the Marquise de la Tour du Pin, a French aristocrat who left France during the Revolution and became a dairy farmer in America; others were more autobiographical. I wrote again and again about my older sister's violent death. But for my most recent novel, I turned to the page to explore my mother's mysterious choices. Perhaps all my books have been attempts to understand them.

It could be that the most precious gift I inherited from my mother, the one which led me to become a writer, was not an object but her silence about so much of her life. It is interesting to note that the word *gift* in German means poison. Sometimes what might seem to take life, like the snake venom, can actually bring it forth. She cloaked herself in folds of mystery, giving us only brief tantalizing glimpses of her true self from time to time. As Friedrich von Hardenberg has said, "Novels arise out of the shortcomings of history." There was so much I didn't know about my mother, this person who should have, after all, been the best known to me, that I felt obliged to turn to the page to attempt to discover it.

What I didn't know about my mother seems symbolized by the little Chinese Buddha that she did bequeath to me. A cheap figurine of a seated Buddha with a bald head, a smiling face, holes for ears, and a large bare stomach, he sits beside me on my desk, grinning implacably despite my shifting moods. In some mysterious way, he reminds me of my mother, with his fixed and inscrutable optimism. When I sit down to work or sometimes in moments of difficulty, I rub his fat stomach — I just did it now again! — for luck.

My mother, like all of us, was complex and mercurial. With the years, she became increasingly secretive and solemn, but as a younger woman she was vivacious, or as she would say, her highest form of praise: "full of beans." As a mother she was most permissive, allowing us great freedom to come and go and do as we wished. This, too, surely was part of her gift to me, the feeling that anything was allowed in life and thus on the page.

When we came back from dances in the evening, she was usually asleep. If she woke, she was eager to find out only if we had been a success, if our dresses had been admired, not at what hour we had come home. "You ought to give us some chores to do," I remember saying gravely. "What chores?" she said, puzzled by this demand.

I can still see her dancing the Charleston barefoot, on the parquet floor, her slim ankles flying in the air, her small beringed hands flapping delicately. She had a great capacity for enjoyment: she loved shopping, pretty clothes, jewelry; she loved to dance, to travel, to eat and drink in large quantities, and above all, to bestow all these good things on those around her. Going through an old trunk I found in my basement recently, I discovered menus from fancy dinners she must have attended with my father, postcards of places all over the world, many with the lines: "We are having a wonderful time." She considered herself lucky, and indeed in many ways was fortunate, and liked to talk about her good luck.

"I have been so lucky all my life," my mother would tell us proudly. She won at the horse races or any other game she chose to play. I think she was referring, too, to marrying my father (again in mysterious circumstances), a wealthy timber merchant who left her a great deal of money at his death when I was just seven years old. Perhaps my father suspected what my mother might do with his fortune, taking care as he did to leave a small portion of it in trust to his two little girls.

Before I discovered some of her secrets, my mother, like the little Buddha, always seemed relentlessly optimistic, always presenting us with a positive image, and keeping the lack of luck in her life hidden, as though it might harm us in some way. Her motto like Candide's seemed to be *"Tout pour le mieux dans le meilleur des mondes."* All is for the best in the best of all worlds.

Rather like a good novelist, she would occasionally confide some small part of the truth to us in a tantalizing way. When my sister and I were twelve and fourteen, she sat us down at the dining room table and confessed rather solemnly that she had something she felt she had to tell us before someone else did. We sat obediently, side by side, at the round table with its bowl of fresh fruit in the center on the crocheted tablecloth, made by my mother who in her youth had done fine sewing, including dressmaking for what she called "pin money."

We had never been treated in this formal fashion before and had no idea what she was about to reveal, though we realized she was nervous. Puzzled and curious, we waited for her to speak. She admitted that when she was seventeen, she had run away to the town of Kimberley and eloped with the love of her life, a young diamond evaluator who worked with her father at De Beers. This was Johannesburg in the twenties.

Instead of being shocked, we were delighted by this romantic story and begged for more details. All she would tell us was that her parents did not approve, as she was so young and particularly as the man, not much older than she, was Jewish. The man's Jewishness in particular delighted us as we had the idea that all Jews were intellectuals, philosophers, writers, or musicians, which we, unlike our mother, aspired to be. Her parents had followed her to Kimberley, the diamond town in the Northern Cape, and had the marriage annulled.

Despite our many questions, she would not divulge more than this: the man was dead now, and he had been the one great love of her life. We were startled by this confession, as she had often told us that the ten years of her marriage to our father were the happiest times of her life. Now, it was clear that our father, a man twenty years older than our mother, who had died years before, had come second in her heart. Had she ever loved him? Had she married him only for his big house and garden, his fortune?

SHE NEVER SPOKE again of this loss or above all of what, decades after her death, I discovered might have been an even greater loss. A few years ago, on a visit to South Africa, my nephew, my sister's only boy, invited my husband and me to lunch. As we sat under an awning in an elegant outdoor

restaurant in the Cape, with its vineyards and blue mountains in the background, my blond-headed nephew lifted his
eyebrows at me significantly, and said that my mother had
stayed in Kimberley after the marriage, with her three maiden
aunts. He paused and then added, "For nine months." I understood immediately, of course, that there must have been
a pregnancy. Perhaps it was at that moment that the seed
for my book was planted, though it took some time to ripen
and come forth. Certainly when I turned to the page, trying
to create imaginatively a life for my mother, to discover why
she had decided to leave her fortune to someone else, I was
filled with sympathy and horror, imagining her as a young
girl, pressured by her family, surely, to stay in seclusion in my
great aunts' house and then to give up her baby.

I knew the house where she had stayed. It had made an
impression on me during a childhood visit to the town of
Kimberley, with its Big Hole, the huge empty crater where
the prospectors had dug and the diamonds had been found.
The three maiden aunts had fluttered around us, stroking
our hair and our skin as though we were something precious
and shining, diamonds perhaps, as we stood shyly in the
half dark of the narrow house with its shotgun passageway
and a fig tree out the back. It was in these reduced circumstances that my mother must have been obliged to hide her
pregnancy, to hush up the scandal, and finally to give up the
child for adoption.

When, almost thirty years after my mother's death, I wrote about this "love child" in a novel, the child was imaginary, though may have, indeed, existed—as my nephew seemed to insinuate. I have never gone to look for this person and have no concrete information of his existence or indeed any certitude that he corresponds to the mysterious man whose name I found in the will. I'm not even sure of the child's sex.

I felt obliged on the page, in order to distance myself from the truth, to change myself and my older sister into two boys who were intellectual snobs, as we were, but who had our father's gift for mathematics rather than our own with words. My sister and I were both avid readers, always immersed in a book while our mother tried to get us to look at life around us. I remember visiting Switzerland as a child and traveling through the snow-clad Alps by train. My mother exhorted us to look out the window, to enjoy the spectacular scenery, but we would not stop reading.

My fictional boys are estranged from their mother. They play chess or puzzle over obscure mathematical conundrums, as we got lost in our eternal books and privileged upbringing. I had felt increasingly distanced from my mother before she died. She was drinking and taking large quantities of pills and had become silent, wrapped in her sorrow. After my sister's brutal death, I felt she had drifted away from the child who remained. Perhaps loving a child, any child, had become too painful for her.

It was only through writing, reaching back into my mother's past as well as my own, that I came to feel closer to my mother, *to feel* sympathy and compassion for this invented woman whose life was filled with *such* sadness and loss. Writing this book enabled me to invent and vicariously relive my mother's life. If Freud is right about our dreams being a fulfilled wish, in some ways even our saddest books fill this purpose as well. In the book, I was able to follow my mother on her imaginary voyage through her young love affair, her marriage to my father, and finally to give her the freedom to leave her money to this girl, the lost child of her youthful passion, someone she had kept a secret, someone as much invented as real.

Through this process, I came to find again the vivacious, loving, generous person who must have been there at the start, long before all she had to leave me were her secrets — the source of much inspiration — and the little smiling Buddha on my desk, a source of hope.

Betrayal

· ·

MARGE PIERCY

My mother married for the first time when she was seventeen to escape a job as chambermaid in a hotel. She had been forced to quit school halfway through the tenth grade in order to bring in money to her poverty-stricken family with too many children to feed. It was a disaster. She was more miserable in that marriage than as a chambermaid being sexually harassed by male travelers.

Her next marriage was to a small businessman with whom she had a son. They were married a number of years. During the Depression, she ran a boardinghouse to help out. There she met my father and eloped with him.

Whatever chemistry they had at first—and it must have been strong—by the time I was born it was gone. It was the marriage of the dog and cat. They could agree on almost nothing. Since he was the breadwinner, he had the power, but she was a great sulker. Although he did pretty much as he pleased — he bought a new car every two years while there was no money for her or me to go to a dentist — she had her own ways of making his life torturous when she chose.

My mother and I were much closer than I ever was to my father, who never got over the disappointment of having a girl and not a boy. My brother came to live with us, and my father preferred him to me, although he was quite harsh with him during his adolescence. I was even more rebellious. Both my brother and I left home as soon as we could.

She had few nice things, but one of them was a jade necklace my father had given her when they eloped. It had an oblong pendant intricately cut on a fine gold chain with smaller globes of green jade set into the links. I seldom saw her wear it. I think she felt few of her clothes were good enough to set it off. But frequently she would take it out, show it to me and hold it, finger it, admire it. Mostly when she was in that nostalgic mood remembering what she chose to cherish from her earlier life, she would go through scraps of velvet or satin or silk from a little chest of drawers stored deep in their closet. The chest was tiny, like something made for a child. She would take out those scraps, recall the dresses they had once been a part of, and tell me some story to go with each. But the prize possession she loved the best was that necklace. She always said as she put it away, "Some day this will be yours."

The last time we spoke on the phone, the Monday before she died suddenly, she reminded me that I was to have it. She seemed afraid that my brother's fourth wife would take it. As she was not ill, I couldn't understand why she brought it up. She suffered a stroke the following week. My husband, Ira, and I flew down on standby the first night of Hanukkah, but my father took her off life support while we were in the air. When we landed, she was already dead.

Along with my brother's wife, I went through her things quickly, as my father intended to get rid of everything. What I took were photographs, my own books signed to her — my father had never read any of them — some shawls I had given her wrapped in plastic and obviously never worn, the rings cut off her fingers by the undertaker, and that jade necklace. She had so little to leave me and I knew how she had cherished it, proof my father had once cared for her. (When I was thirteen, she made a fuss about wanting a present from him for her birthday. He bought her a kitchen garbage can.) I told him I was taking it, to make sure he did not mind. He claimed never to have seen it before and denied having given it to her.

I put it on now and then, always reminded of her, always missing her freshly. Two years after my mother's death, I was invited to a party on Labor Day weekend and decided to wear it. It was not in my jewelry box. I was frightened. How could I have misplaced or lost it? I always put it away carefully in the exact front left-hand corner of the upper drawer. I took everything out. I crawled all over the floor. I tried to remember the last time I had worn it, about six weeks earlier. Had I not put it away? But I always did. Always. I had a stomachache all day. Obviously I had done something stupid with it. Ever since my mother died, I had been misplacing things. I saw it as a metaphor, that since I had lost her, I kept losing other things, especially clothing and jewelry.

Monday, Labor Day, I received a phone call. It was from the roommate of my assistant, who had been working for me for seven years. Two and a half years earlier my assistant's marriage had broken up and she had been briefly homeless. I let her stay in my house while I was in Florida for my mother's funeral. Earlier that year, my assistant had complained of pains and gone to her gynecologist, who told her nothing was wrong with her except nerves. From her symptoms I did not believe he was correct. I suspected she had an ectopic pregnancy. I made an appointment with her at a women's clinic in Boston. Her pains got worse. When she arrived and was examined, they discovered I was correct and that her situation was critical. They rushed her into an operating room and saved her life.

Her roommate was very nervous but said she felt she had

to tell me that my assistant had been stealing from me with some regularity for the past two years. At first, the roommate said, she had taken little things when she was staying in my house. But it had escalated. The roommate felt some of the objects were too precious for me not to miss them, including a jade necklace my assistant had been boasting about. I told her I'd come over that evening.

The roommate let us into my assistant's room. I began going through her things. I didn't care if she arrived or not. I didn't care if what I was doing was legal or not. I found the necklace very quickly and in fear that somehow it would disappear, I put it on. I found other jewelry of mine, including a gold Mogen David my husband had given me. My assistant was not Jewish. I also found all the clothes, the watch, the other items I thought I had misplaced or lost. I collected them all. Her roommate told me my assistant had developed a cocaine habit over the past year. She was spending the night with a man she had met recently in a bar and planned to go to work directly from his apartment.

When she arrived Tuesday morning, I was wearing the jade necklace. I confronted her. I had put all the items I had recovered from her bedroom in a pile on the table. She kept saying her mother had given her the jade necklace and her boyfriend had given her the Mogen David. She wept. I told her she was fired and I would not prosecute her but never wanted to see her again. She stopped crying, picked up her purse and started out.

She turned. "Does that mean you won't give me a letter of recommendation?"

I still have my mother's jade necklace, and every time I touch it and every time I put it on, I think of her and I still miss her. I don't think missing a mother ever stops. I have decided to be buried with it.

The Silver in the Salt Air

ELEANOR CLIFT

I don't have many material things from my mother, Inna Josine Jappen Roeloffs — she wasn't a material girl. She was an immigrant from the tiny island of Föhr in the North Sea off Germany and Denmark, who came to America at nineteen years old in 1923, newly married to my father, who was ten years older than she was. Seasick all the way, she came through Ellis Island, and told me once that she would never have agreed to the journey if she'd known it would be for good. But she put any regrets aside to create a life with my father, working with him in the delicatessen they owned together, initially in Brooklyn, and then, during most of my growing up, in Queens.

She made the potato salad, rice pudding, and custard, her hands so callous that she could peel potatoes moments after they came out of boiling water. What she did looked easy but of course it wasn't. That was true of a lot of the life lessons she passed down to me, including her instructions on how to make a marriage work, and specifically her marriage to my father, Erk Diedrich Roeloffs. He was the classic in-charge German male, impatient and always barking orders. On the surface, my mother was a deferential housewife, but she shared her secret weapon with me when I was still a girl: "Do what you want to do. Just don't talk about it." She really ran the show; he just didn't know it. Pop would say no; Mom would wait awhile, and soon all would be well.

Americanizing his first name to Ed, my father dealt with the customers out front while my mother rarely ventured from the wood-floored kitchen in the back of the store. She was a very hard worker, and paid no attention to fashion. She wore what were then called housedresses, cotton prints that she usually bought off the rack from neighborhood stores—the racks displayed on the sidewalk—without even trying them on. Today, Indian sarees hang outside those shops in Jackson Heights, Queens, where we moved after the war, when I was five.

Mom wore sturdy shoes with wedge heels, and I don't remember any makeup in the house, except an occasional lipstick for church on Sunday. But she had a stash of jewelry that I knew was special even as a young girl, yet she never wore any of the pieces and kept them wrapped in soft material in a dresser drawer as you would keep precious silverware. By the time I saw the jewelry she had brought with her from Europe, she had been in her adoptive country for more than two decades. The horrors of World War II had ended their visits to the German-owned North Sea island she called home, and when she occasionally took out the dozen or so pieces to polish them, she told me that in the salt air of the island, they didn't tarnish the way they did in America. It was a prideful comparison, one of the few she could find in those postwar years.

More through indirection than anything she said, I knew her jewelry would be mine. As the only daughter, with brothers ten and sixteen years older, it was up to me to carry on the tradition represented by this collection. As a teenager, I was pretty blasé about anything having to do with my parents' native land. I wanted to be American, and this odd, faraway place held no allure for me. Mom would tuck the items away, confident that I would someday appreciate what she was setting aside.

She was right—my attitude changed when I became an adult with a family of my own. I can't remember exactly when I got her jewelry because there was no fanfare. But by the time she died at age sixty-nine with her mind fogged from Alzheimer's disease, I was grateful to have these tangible symbols of a heritage and a culture that Mom had feared would be lost in America.

This distinctively silver jewelry with its delicate lattice design is known throughout Germany as belonging to Föhr and two neighboring islands, Amrum and Sylt, where it is part of the traditional costume women and girls wear for special occasions. I have a picture taken of me in the ceremonial garb when I was in my twenties, on my first visit to Föhr and pregnant with my second child. I'm wearing a long basic black dress borrowed from a cousin and covered from the waist down by a lacy-looking white apron. Round buttonlike baubles, exact replicas of my mother's jewels, rest like a half-moon cloak of silver on my bodice. To refresh my memory of forty years ago, I googled Föhr, and watched with enchantment images of Föhr's finest in traditional dress.

I felt awkward standing there as relatives I barely knew debated in Föhring (yes, the island has its very own language) whom I most resembled, as though I were just an assemblage of genes passing through the generations. At the time, I was not yet a journalist. I was working as a "Girl Friday" in the Atlanta bureau of *Newsweek*. It was 1969, and we had just gone through the assassinations of Dr. Martin Luther King Jr. and Bobby Kennedy. I had one son and another on the way, and it was comforting to know that amid such turbulence, a place like Föhr existed, beckoning me back to a simpler time and place, with thatched-roof houses and cobblestone streets.

We took my mother back to Föhr the winter of 1972. She wanted to go home, and she died the following summer in a nursing home on the island. By then, I had her jewelry, along with some similar pieces from a favorite aunt who never married and had moved back to Föhr. I keep them in a small luminous blue box that sits on my dresser and that has a clear top so I can see the contents. The box is so perfect I'd like to think it's an heirloom, but on the corner of the lid it says COVERGIRL, which makes it a vintage collectible, and quite American.

Note to burglars: The jewelry looks antique, and it is old, but it is not especially valuable. The largest piece is a silver lattice pendant with a large yellow-gold gemstone set in the middle, which Mom told me was a gift from my father to mark their engagement. That didn't strike me as odd at the time, but studying the amber stone later and trying to understand the symbolism, I thought it must be my mother's birthstone. But no, I discovered the honey-toned gem marks the month of November, which is when my father was born; my mother had a January birthday. Maybe he just liked it. Whatever the reason, my mother cherished it, and it's about the only thing I remember her telling me was a gift from him that wasn't purely practical.

Mom often repeated that silver never tarnishes in the salt air of the island, only here in America. She's right that it is darker here, but I'm not sure it's immune to tarnish in its native habitat. She once told me that everyone on the island is blond, like me, and when I was there, I could see for myself that while there were plenty of blonds, there were darker-haired people, too. "Oh, they're tourists," my mother said. That was her story, and she was sticking to it.

Having this jewelry brings the Old World to me along with the strength of my mother, who left her family while still in her teens to marry a man who at twenty-nine had set his course in life. He took her across the ocean to New York, a place bigger and scarier than anything she could have imagined, and where she didn't know the language. But she did it, and she built a good life, later showing the same grit and fortitude in learning how to drive at age sixty after my father died. I think of the courage that took, and it helps me in meeting life's challenges to know I've got her DNA.

Like my mother, I hardly ever wear the jewelry, but it beckons to me from its blue box. All it takes is a glance, and I can feel a powerful connection to the tiny windswept island in the North Sea, and to the woman who gave me life.

While the jewelry represents the continuity of my unique heritage, the other item that my mother didn't intend to give me but that I think of as a gift from her, is much more mundane. It was a can of Johnson Paste Wax that she kept in a mesh bag in the car for her visits to my father's grave out near Kennedy Airport, so she could polish the marker. She went every week, and as I think about it, that was probably why she learned how to drive. For me, it was a powerful lesson in love and loyalty, and the enduring gestures that matter.

She Gave Me the World

·····································

MARY MORRIS

I'm driving with a friend into Rome. We zip past Roman pines, cypresses that dot the hillsides. The golden Mediterranean light filters down. Its brightness illumines the ruins of aqueducts and walls as we drive on the old Via Appia. I'd been teaching in Umbria for the past week and now I'm on vacation. I know Rome well. In some ways it is my city. I've visited many times and lived here for a year. I know my way around. I know what to avoid. Still I find myself sitting at the top of the Via Veneto at Harry's Bar, sipping wine. Normally I'd avoid this part of town. It's touristy and expensive. But it's where my friend wanted to be.

As we sit, chatting, I look across the street and see the Hotel Flora. I'd forgotten about the Flora and am surprised to see

that it's still there. Though it's been almost fifty years since
I've seen, or even really given much thought to the Flora, I
suddenly recall every moment I once spent here as a girl. "I
stayed in that hotel," I tell my friend. "It's still there." She
nods, grimacing as she tastes her bitter Campari. At dusk my
friend must meet someone for dinner, and I decide to wander
alone. I cross the street. I peer inside the lobby. I contemplate
going in, but then I might have to answer a question or two
and I don't particularly want to.

Instead I head through the ancient Porta Pinciana, past
the crumbling Aurelian walls, and cut over to the Villa Borghese gardens. Here I leave the bustle of the city behind.
In the gardens it is quiet and cool as I stroll on a tree-lined
path. Pausing among the tall pines, I take out my phone,
and call my mother to tell her where I am. "I'm in Italy," I
say, "in Rome. Do you remember the Hotel Flora? Do you
remember when you brought me here?" But on the other end
of the phone my mother grows confused. She tells me her
knees hurt, but otherwise she is fine. She doesn't remember
the Flora or Rome. "Italy?" she asks, her mind struggling to
recall. And I can tell that she doesn't even know what Italy is
anymore. "Remember our trip?" I ask her. "You threw your
pearls into the sea."

My mother, of course, is fading. She is ninety-nine years
old, and I have watched her world shrink. Just a few years
ago she was still talking about us going once more to Paris.

Then it was Montreal. And Chicago, the city where she lived her entire life until, in their nineties, my parents moved to Milwaukee to be near my brother. But when I was a sullen teenager in love with the Irish boy who lived on the other side of the tracks (quite literally), my mother picked me up one day after school. "Get in the car," she said. "We're going to get your passport." I didn't want a passport. I didn't even know what one was really. My summer would revolve around only these things: learning to touch type and spending every free afternoon at the beach and in the arms of the boy I loved.

But my mother had other plans for me. As we drove south on Edens from the suburbs where we lived, to downtown Chicago, she explained that she intended to take me to Paris, London, and Rome as soon as school let out. She had never been anywhere except to Idaho one summer—a place she detested. And she was longing to travel. Anyone who knew my mother knew this about her.

When I was much younger, my parents were invited to a Suppressed Desire Ball. You were to come in a costume that depicted your secret wish, your heart's desire. My mother went into a kind of trance and for weeks our pool table was covered in blue taffeta, white fishnet gauze, travel posters, and brochures as she began to construct on her seamstress's mannequin the most extraordinary costume I've ever seen.

Sometimes I'd go downstairs to watch her, sewing, cutting late into the night. "What do you think about the Taj

Mahal?" "Where should the pyramids go?" On and on into the night my mother pasted and sewed. The night of the ball my father looked dashing in his tuxedo and toupee (he was going as a man with hair), but it was my mother who entranced me. Within her blue skirts, she had sewn pictures of the Great Wall of China, the Eiffel Tower. On her head sat an aluminum globe. Her skirts were the oceans. Her body the land. And laced between the layers were Tokyo, Istanbul, Tashkent. Instead of seeing the world, my mother became it.

Now she wanted to do the grand tour of Europe. And I was appalled. "Can't Dad go?" I whined. We both knew that my father never would. He hated to go anywhere except to his office, the golf course, or a bridge table. I was to be her reluctant companion, an accidental tourist for six weeks on the road. This was, at the time, my worst nightmare. "I don't want to," I told her, staring out as the flat, Midwestern landscape sped by.

My mother gripped the wheel with her white gloves. "You're going," she said.

The passport office was located in a dreary green institutional-type building. Inside, my mother took a number, got some forms, and sat down in a gray plastic chair. As we waited, a woman in some kind of military uniform entered. She wore high boots and a cap and began to stomp around, then gave the *Sieg Heil* salute to me, clicking her heels together. I was terrified, but my mother laughed. "It's awful, I know," my mother said. "But she's just crazy." Still this woman made me feel that the world I was about to enter was a dangerous place, and I was its reluctant visitor.

A few weeks later, a thick, official-looking envelope arrived which my mother handed to me with a flourish, as if I were being anointed for something. But for what? Inside I found my navy blue passport with the gold seal of the United States on its cover. I flipped through its blank, virgin pages, then tucked it into the passport case my mother had given me with my initials inscribed. I didn't really give this passport much thought. Nor did I understand its secret powers until we arrived in Paris, early on a Saturday morning, groggy from sleep, and the French customs official in his dark blue uniform and high red hat raised his stamp and imprinted it onto my passport. He handed it back to me and welcomed me to France. I had crossed my first border.

We stayed in the Hotel Vendome. My mother loved its mahogany canopied beds, its red damask curtains. She savored peach melba in the evenings and washed her feet in the bidet. Paris had long been a dream of my mother's. She'd named our first dog Renoir. When I was in grammar school, she insisted that I learn French. (In fact before I graduated from high school, my mother saw to it that all the grammar schools in our town offered French by the sixth grade.) Every Tuesday afternoon, I went over to see poor Monsieur LaTate who had a nervous tic and seemed despondent as I struggled with the irregular verbs. And I was pretty miserable, too.

But my mother was adamant. She was a Midwestern housewife who probably belonged more in a salon than a supermarket. She had a certificate in fashion design from the Art Institute of Chicago, and her idol was Coco Chanel. In the 1930s, when my mother was working at Saks, selling ladies underwear, a big designer came in to show the saleswomen how to dress the mannequin. As he was trying to explain something that no one seemed able to grasp, my mother held up the sketch she'd just drawn. "Is this what you mean?" He asked her how she learned to do that. My mother just shrugged. "I taught myself," she said.

The designer helped my mother get a scholarship to the Art Institute of Chicago, where she studied fashion until her father refused to give her the carfare she needed to get to school. But she still designed and made all her own clothes. If there was one battle my mother and I fought over and over (down to my own wedding gown), it was how I looked and what I wore. Once she gave me sixty dollars to buy new clothes, and when I got home and tried them on, she took them all back. I remember putting on a little yellow short and shirt set. "Yellow is not your color," my mother said.

She quickly fell in love with Paris. During the day, my mother dressed to perfection in her dark suit with black patent leather pumps, white gloves, and always her strand of cultured pearls. They were a rather cheap strand—something she often complained about—but she wore them everywhere as we clomped around Paris, where she searched for eyeliners and perfumes (Chanel No. 5, Réplique, of which she bought boxes to take home), handbags, and shoes. She didn't care what anything cost. "So broke, so broke," she used to say. We were at this time in our lives "comfortable." This was not to last forever, but on this trip she didn't bat an eye as she bought me a royal blue cloth coat to match my eyes ("Definitely your color"). She dragged me to every Monet and monument she could find. We climbed the steps of Montmartre and found a little bistro where, for the first time, I sipped wine, then staggered back to the hotel. We dined on the Seine on a bateau *mouche* with Paris illumined all around us. My mother didn't just visit Paris. She drank it in.

Then we went on to Rome. We stayed at the Flora—the hotel that has made me recall this journey now—in a plush room with a sofa and a view of the Via Veneto. I'm sure Marcello Mastroianni passed us in the street. A handsome, young doorman, who must be an old man by now, called me Miss America and flirted with me in a way that I think my mother found secretly charming. "How is Miss America? Where is Miss America going today?" And we were going everywhere. For the first days, we hired a guide who took us all over Rome. It seemed as if my mother never wanted to stop. When he mentioned that he was taking us to the oldest market in Rome, she asked what she could buy there. "I wouldn't know, Madame," he replied in his broken English. "It's been closed for two thousand years."

My mother was enchanted with it all. The street sign SENSO UNICO, which she thought was the name of our street (as opposed to the Via Veneto). The audience we had with the pope and about five thousand other people at the Vatican. The nuns who shoved to get past us. The priest from Chicago who led us by the hand. One afternoon, we went across the street to the famous Eva of Rome, where we had our hair done. Mine was washed, set, and combed into a fluffy confection that was then sprayed. I hated it. My handsome doorman gave me a wink. "Miss America, what have you done to your hair?" he asked as I walked by.

Back in our room, my mother lay down to take a nap. When she was sound asleep, I stuck my head in the sink, combed it out, and towel dried it back to a semblance of its former self. Then I set out on my own. Leaving the hotel, I crossed over to the Villa Borghese gardens, happy to be alone, walking in the shade. But it was not long before I began to hear sharp whistles, the sounds of men calling. Some followed, shouting "Bella!" And other things I didn't understand. It took me a few minutes to understand that these catcalls were for me. I was both frightened and entranced. I found myself being coaxed into this world of strange men, and my Irish boy back home suddenly paled. Though I didn't know what they were saying, I did understand that I was on the brink of something and my life was about to change.

I bid sad good-bye to my doorman, saying I'd send him a postcard (which I'm not sure I ever did), and we traveled on to Florence. As we left Rome, the bus driver's wife handed him a lunch pail and clean clothes. As they kissed good-bye, he cradled her face in his hands in a loving way. "Italians are so romantic," my mother said. As we rode along, I gazed out at ruins and cypresses, the vineyards and olive trees, until we stopped at a small town. Here another woman greeted our driver with a kiss and, as he went off to spend his lunch break with her, my mother laughed and laughed. "I don't get it," I said.

"Oh you will. One day you will."

Florence, Pisa, Genoa. We bussed across Italy. We were heading to Nice, but en route, stopped for a night in a seaside town of La Spezia. On a warm summer evening we sat, dining on a balcony with the sea stretching before us. With the sun still shining, we dined on grilled fish and sipped cold white wine. It was, I would have to say, kind of a perfect moment. And here my mother put her hands on the strand of cultured pearls she'd worn for years. As the waiter came to clear, she unwound it over her head. "I'm sick of these," she said. And with that, she tossed them into the sea. The waiter and I watched, aghast, as they sank into the Mediterranean, disappearing from view. I had no idea what to say. I just stared at my mother, stunned. Then we both began to laugh. I recognized then what I've come to know is true. Travel can be transformative.

My mother has given me many things over the years—jewelry, china, silver. A few years ago, she handed me her mink coat (which I have worn once). These things never meant very much to me—perhaps because they meant so much to her. But I recall that first passport, holding it in my hands. I remember the moment the French customs official placed a stamp in its virgin pages and welcomed me to France. I cannot say that my mother and I have always had a smooth ride, but out of all that she has given me, or tried to give or pawn off, it is my passport and the world it opened up for me that has been the greatest gift. My mother set me off on a journey and I have yet to stop.

Since then, I have wandered through Latin America, traveled from Beijing to Berlin by rail, searched for tigers in the jungles of India. And now I am back in Rome. I stand in the Villa Borghese gardens as the golden light of evening filters down, and my mother tells me she's tired and wants to get off the phone. Then she asks as she always does, "When am I going to see you?" "Soon, Mommy," I tell her, "I'll be there soon." Beside a pond, lovers kiss, their bodies entwined on park benches. Boats row in the waning sunlight. A family of ducks paddles past as my mother ends our conversation the way she always does. She tells me she loves me with all her heart. There was a time in my life when I wasn't sure what the heart was, but I feel clearer as I grow older.

I get off the phone and wander through the gardens. I snap pictures. I sit down on a park bench in the same gardens where I once walked. And now I open my laptop and hook up to free Wi-Fi. Dappled light filters down. The Roman pines soar above me. When I was a girl, I thought these were a unique species of tree. It wasn't until I was much older that I learned that the Italians trim them this way—with no branches along the trunk, but bushy on the top. It is a paradox perhaps only Italians understand. You can keep the shade and still let the light in. And beneath the canopy, I see myself, my much younger self, avoiding the Italian men who call to me as I stroll among the shadows.

A Thousand Words a Day
and One Charming Note

· ·

LISA SEE

My mother, Carolyn See, is a writer. Her father was a writer. And now I'm a writer. My mother's best gift was the advice she gave me not just long ago but nearly every day since then: "Write a thousand words a day and one charming note."

When I was a little girl, my mom was in graduate school at UCLA, getting her PhD in English. She read to me the usual kids' books, as well as what she was reading for her courses. (I could be wrong, but I don't think *The Old Man and the Sea* is a typical bedtime story for a five-year-old.) My mom wanted to be a writer. She thought it would change her life, and it did. But it wasn't easy for her. Fifty years ago, there weren't many women writers who were being published. And there certainly weren't many women writers on the West Coast who were seeing their work in print either. I used to eavesdrop when she spoke with magazine editors on the phone, listening to how she would answer their mindless or impertinent queries and riveted by her strength and composure even when she was completely irritated with those men (back then editors were mostly men) on the other end of the line. I looked on as she revised articles, profiles, and books. I went with her sometimes when she interviewed people and listened to her caustic retelling of some of the idiotic things celebrities, such as James Garner, Linda Lovelace, and Carol Burnett, felt compelled to confide to a journalist. I heard her say to herself almost as a mantra, "A thousand words a day and one charming note," time and time again. Many years later, when I was looking through her papers at UCLA Special Collections, I came across a letter from her father in which he said that the only way to become a real writer was to write a thousand words a day, *no matter what.*

Maybe it's the *no matter what* that's the key. When I was growing up, I watched my mother curl up on the couch in our little house at the top of a steep and isolated hill in Topanga Canyon, open a black Flair pen, and then write a thousand words on a plain white pad of paper, every day, no matter what—even when my stepfather ran off with another woman, when brush fires burned around us, when the world told her that she couldn't get published, when some awful editor in a skyscraper three thousand miles away was so mean that after one of those dreaded phone conversations she'd go in the bathroom and cry, and when my baby sister wailed and I sulked and pouted like only a petulant teenager can. I also watched my mom write charming notes to editors at magazines and publishing houses. These weren't just any notes. These notes made me squirm not only from the audacity that she was writing to people who were so important but also for the nerve of what she put down on her pretty stationery with her black Flair pen.

"They don't know who we are," she explained. "We have to let them know we're out here. That this is *the* place. That we are *the* ones." She was bold, fearless, impudent, and endlessly funny in her notes. Who was chosen to be a recipient of a charming note? If his name made your hands sweat, then he earned a note. "I'll stop by your office to meet with you about some story ideas on March 3 at two o'clock," she might write to someone she'd never met or spoken to, say, the editor in chief of *Esquire* or some other big-deal magazine of the day. She wasn't begging for an audience. She was just stating a fact in a positive way. Most times the editor would call and say, "Yes, come on by. I'll see you at two. Or would you rather have lunch? You live in Topanga Canyon, right? We've been so curious about what's been happening there . . ." But if he didn't respond quickly and with gusto, then my mom would send flowers or balloons or bottles of California wine until he did. She got a lot of her early magazine assignments on chutzpah and good cheer, but I have to say her notes weren't always

charming. After one bitter rejection, she waited several months
and then boxed up some of our goat's droppings and mailed
them off to that snippy New York editor.

When people asked me, "Do you want to be a writer like
your mother?" the answer was a big fat *NO*. It was too terrifying and disheartening to me and, at the time, I didn't see
the rewards. I didn't want to be on the receiving end of those
editing phone calls. I didn't want to be rejected. I couldn't
see myself persisting in the face of great odds.

But here's the thing: I may have said I didn't want to be a
writer, but my mom included me in the process from the time
I was about thirteen. She showed me everything she wrote —
from the smallest magazine article to all ten of her book
manuscripts — to read and edit. What on earth did I, a sullen teenager, have to offer my mother in the way of editing?
In those early days, I honestly don't know. Even today I don't
know where the comma goes. But as she recalled the other
day, "I trusted you. You were in the house. It was just you,
your sister, and me against the world. Who else was there?"
My mother taught me to look for words and phrases that get
repeated, notice holes in the plot, and beware inconsistencies
in a character. My mom was giving me the gift of words.
What words work? What words are too powerful to be used
more than once in 350 pages? What makes a character —
whether real or imagined — do the things she does? How do
you get a character from her front door to her car and on to
her big adventure? I was my mom's apprentice, even though

I didn't realize it back then. And still I claimed I didn't want to be a writer.

When I was nineteen, I left college and went off to Europe with a boyfriend. I thought I knew certain things about myself: I didn't want to be a writer, I didn't want to get married, I didn't want to have children, and I always wanted to live out of a suitcase. The big question with this imagined life was how I would support myself. I kept pondering this as I bummed around Europe on five dollars a day. Finally, we rented a small house on the island of Patmos for thirty-five dollars a month. Still, I was thinking, *How will I be able to pay for this "free" life I've envisioned for myself?* Then, one morning, I woke up and it was like a lightbulb had flashed on in my brain. *Oh, I could be a writer!*

When I returned home many months later, I got my first two magazine assignments within forty-eight hours. A miracle, right? No, my mother gave me those, too. When a magazine called her and asked her to write a piece about sex on the college campus, she said that she didn't want to write it, but she knew who would be perfect—her daughter, who was just going back to college and had some experience on the topic. When an editor from a start-up sports magazine called and asked if she'd like to write for them, she said that she hated sports, which is true, but that her daughter loved sports, which was a lie, and that I would be perfect. She even suggested the topic: an article about my former stepfather's new wife, who then held the record in the woman's marathon.

Somewhere in there, my relationship with my boyfriend fell apart, and I moved into my mom's new house in To-panga. My rent? Ten percent of everything I earned. I was making something like five cents a word, but my mom didn't care. She was acting as my agent and teaching me to be a professional. So there we were — my mom, my little sister, and the newly arrived John Espey, the big love of my mom's life. Summer in Topanga is brutal. And we were all broke. One night we were watching a really bad miniseries on tele-vision. We looked at each other, and someone said, "We could do better than this." That was the birth of Monica Highland — a pseudonym for my mom, John, and me. We wrote three books together. I held the pen and we all talked. John was a Rhodes scholar, my mom was a PhD, and I was the apprentice. We drank Château Topanga Champagne and laughed ourselves silly.

A thousand words a day and one charming note encom-passes more than just those two tasks. My mother and I talk either in person or on the phone nearly every day about what we're working on, but also about editors, editing, bookstores, promotion, publicity, book tours, and just about every facet of what's happening in the world of publishing on any given day. And then there's the writing itself.

My mom was in the hospital recently. What was supposed to be minor surgery with a four-day admission turned into a twelve-day stay. We had lots of time to kill, and so we talked and talked. Inevitably, the conversation always came back to writing. "Suffering is the only authentic emotion," she said one afternoon. We considered that idea for hours — how it affects us in our daily lives and how it's played out in our writing. On another day, we talked about motherhood. I said that to me motherhood is about sacrifice, courage, and loyalty. She laughed, and said she didn't have any of those traits. She was in the hospital, so I wasn't going to argue with her, but she was absolutely wrong. She's shown me that to be a woman, a mother, or a writer I must sacrifice, show courage, and be loyal. I must look for those authentic emotions. I can never give up or bow to people who tell me that I can't write because I'm a woman, that no one cares what I have to say, or that I'm worthless.

And if you think my worries are senseless in this day and age, then think again. Consider the balance of male writers to female writers on best-seller lists or how women writers are still paid far less than men. On a more personal level, I'll just say that the editor for my first book was very cruel and wrote things in the margins like, "What kind of a vacuous person would write a sentence like this?" It takes courage to write *deep* and it takes even more courage to fight to have your voice heard, even now.

Today my mother is considered the grande dame of West Coast letters. Sometimes I allow myself to step back, look at her in that way, and celebrate her accomplishments. But usually, she's still my mom.

Then There Must Be a Story

· ·

ELIZABETH BENEDICT

"What a pretty scarf," people often say when I'm buttoning my winter coat and it's draped around the collar, about to be knotted at my neck against the cold. "Where did you get it?"

"My mother gave it to me," I begin and mumble the rest, disappointed the answer is so inelegant, and that I don't have a shopping tip to offer: "She bought it from a vendor at the assisted-living place where she lived." I'm more than disappointed that I don't know where to buy another if I lose it, the last gift my mother ever gave me, two or three years before she died. Twice I couldn't find it—once when she was still alive and once after. The second time, I went into a full-fledged panic, the sort I feel when I think I've lost my purse.

It's a six-foot-long piece of black wool cloth, more than a

foot wide when extended, made in India, and decorated at each end with a wide band of embroidered flowers in yellow, gold, light pink, and light blue threads. It's the vibrant pastel-colored stitching, the way it stands out against the black, that catches the eye so often. The flowers are boxy and stylized, not real looking, and I have never seen another scarf like it.

Last winter, getting ready to leave a restaurant, a woman I don't know well paid it a compliment and asked where it came from. "My mother gave it to me," was all I said, but she must have heard something in my voice — something tentative.

"Oh, your mother," she said kindly. "Then there must be a story."

THE STORY IS her sad story and my sad story, and the tender place where these stories collide — or do they run together? Are we like oil and water or like the cream in each other's coffee? My sister would not have to wonder which metaphor to pick. She was crazy for my mother, loved and needed her unquestioningly all her life, all the more so, since her relationship to our father was miserable. He was short-tempered and she snapped at him; he bullied and she bullied back. My mother was her life raft. There was altogether too much fighting in the family, and I was the one who checked out at an early age: precocious, bored, eager to find other families that suited me better, and independent in the way of New York City kids. I picked out an alternate mother when I was nine years old: she was bold and beautiful and lived in a fittingly glamorous apartment downstairs from ours. It would be years before the irony of my choice became apparent to me; alcohol ruined her—and her own mothering—many times over.

Detaching came easily to me. I'm not as high-strung as my sister, and my father and I had a few good years when I was young, before alcoholic nastiness seeped into his pores. And there was this: my father was ambitious and nervy and out in the world, where he wanted to be very successful—and was, for quite a few years. My mother was nice, meek, depressed, and abjectly in love with him. She was a gifted painter and had gone to art school instead of college, but painting, and then sculpting, would always be a hobby, a passion she could sometimes make time for while trying mightily, in later years, to support herself. I didn't particularly need her to protect me from our father, as my sister did, so it was easier for me to want to be more like him than like her: strong, not weak; nervy, not gloomy; cynical, not sentimental.

We were a 1950s-style nuclear family. When my mother got up the nerve to leave him when I was thirteen, she took my sister and me with her back to our hometown far from Manhattan. When she returned to him a few weeks later, having lost her nerve, we knew that he, not she, was the bad guy. Five years

later, when they were about to call it quits, my sister and I
cheered her on, encouraged her to finally make the break,
even though she knew he would not help her financially—
and she was right. Though the last thing I wanted was to
become a woman like my mother, it was not possible to take
his side in our domestic dramas.

I KEPT MY distance from both of them. I moved
to California and changed my name, had a ton of therapy,
moved back East, wrote several novels that were—beneath
a kind of surface glitter and glibness—fundamentally about
women who had a hard time expressing their deepest feelings. Once I got through those, there were several other novels about people in crisis—very fictionalized versions of the
crises in my own life. The mothers in my novels, though, had
no relation to my mother, except in a later one, where she has
a walk-on part as a mom losing her memory, which seemed
generic enough to mask the more complicated truth.

She didn't appear in my fiction because I had no way to
describe—or do I mean to disguise?—the distance I felt
from her. When certain popular books or magazine articles
about mothers came to my attention, it didn't occur to me
to read them. I no more identified with the community of
women and their mothers than I identified with Queen Noor
of Jordan—an American woman about my age who had
grown up in the United States and then married a Middle

Eastern king. Sure, we had come from the same place—but we ended up on different planets. When I looked around at my closest women friends, almost every one had a tragic mother story, one more heartbreaking and unbelievable than the next. I knew I was comfortable with women who'd had damaged mothers, mothers who had never been quite all there for them.

And when it came to the matter of my wanting or not wanting to be a mother myself, I wavered for years. During the childbearing years in which I was married, I always had a book to finish; when I decided I wanted a child, I was in my late thirties. We tried for several years, and attempted various kinds of intervention. Had things happened naturally, I would have been a mother. But when I had to choose between injecting myself with weeks of hormones every month or not, I chose not to. When I had to choose between adopting a daughter—the social worker called to tell me one was available—and leaving an unhappy marriage, I left the marriage and gave up the quest for my own child. Since then, I've been lucky in that department. I now have a wonderful stepdaughter and a wonderful niece who is like a daughter, since her own mother, my sister-in-law, died three years ago. Better still, these young women are first cousins, and close. Very lucky indeed.

But it did not escape my notice that when the choice was mine, I eschewed motherhood. Other women I know took hormones for years, adopted when marriages were falling apart, adopted without marriage. I wanted to be a mother—but not in that all-out fashion. In 2004, after my parents were both gone, I shucked the disguises of fiction and began research-ing and writing a long essay about a famous murder in my mother's family that happened months before my parents got married. I spent a year on it, and in the course of those investigations into my mother's past and my own, I came to understand the other reason I had felt such ambivalence about having children of my own: at some very deep level, I didn't want anyone I loved as much as I knew I would love a child to feel as remote from me as I'd felt from my mother; I didn't want anyone to want to flee from me as I'd wanted to flee from her. It was a shocking realization, and it explained a lot.

WHEN MY MOTHER began to lose her memory in a drastic way, and we moved her in with her sister, to an assisted-living community in White Plains, my sister was devastated by the loss. She asked me often how I felt, hoping for company. Mom now is like Mom before, I said, only more so. Then and now, she had not been there for me. She and my sister liked to shop for clothes, and I didn't. They didn't care about the news, and I did. Before, when I visited my mother in her apartment, I didn't know what to talk to her about. I tried to be dutiful, to be nice, generous, the things she wanted me to be, what is expected of a grown daughter with a kind, needy mother who worried about money and sent checks for a dollar to nearly every charity that solicited her. We shopped for food, watched TV, visited her friends, and went to the shop in her little town that displayed her beautiful marble sculptures, pieces my sister and I were happy to inherit. Often the visits felt like a strain to me, but I hope they did not to her; they are a strain to remember because I wish I could rewrite them, wish I had been closer, kinder, more easygoing, more comfortable — though maybe, just maybe, she had no complaints. Maybe I was the one with all the complaints.

At the assisted-living place — a quasi-luxury apartment building in downtown White Plains — my mother and aunt were sociable and well taken care of. I was in charge of their finances, and I visited often. It must have been her first Hanukkah there that my mother gave me the beautiful scarf, purchased from a vendor who probably spent a day or two selling jewelry and holiday tchotchkes to the residents. I don't remember the moment she gave it to me, whether it was wrapped, what she said. I just started wearing it around the collar of my navy coat and getting compliments quite often. The wool isn't heavy but it's long enough so that I can wrap it several times around my neck and halfway up my face, and it's real protection against the cold.

The more I wore it and the more compliments I got, the more attached to it I became. I couldn't think of another gift she had given me in years that I had liked as much — that was as pretty or as useful. I was not "into clothes" but this was beautiful. I never wore pastels, but these pastel threads were stunning against the black wool. And the scarf was there all winter long, keeping me warm.

The scarf didn't literally glitter but it had a glittering effect, or so it felt to me. It caught people's attention often for many months every year, for the next three years in which my mother declined, and then declined precipitously. She was ten years younger than her sister, but she died a year before. It is painful to remember the years after she gave me the scarf, the journey from the assisted-living building to the nursing home, from the floor of "OK" residents to the floor of the decidedly not OK. I spent a lot of time visiting her and my aunt, who remained on the OK floor until she died. I can't bear to remember the actual names of the floors, the conditions they referred to.

Before the worst of it, visiting was heartbreaking, but also strangely tranquilizing. I sometimes stayed for hours, just sitting with my mother and aunt watching TV, eating meals, sometimes taking my mother to the art studio, or walking past the electric train set and into the gardens that overlooked the Hudson River. There were musicians who came to sing and play the piano, and a kindly rabbi who conducted services and knew everyone's name.

One of the last times I pushed my mother's wheelchair to the end of the hall, to take in the breathtaking view of the George Washington Bridge over the water, it was late afternoon and the sky was a dozen shades of orange. "Liz, did you make that?" my mother asked. She meant the landscape she saw against the window—a modern-day Hudson River School canvas. She still knew my name, but she had me mistaken for a painter—when she was the painter in the family.

"No, Mom, God made that." It was not what I usually thought or said about landscape or anything else, but it must have made sense in that moment.

THE YEARS OF caretaking softened my hard edges and rubbed away a lifetime of distance between us, and the scarf, the beautiful scarf that everyone notices and asks about, does a motherly job year in and year out: protects, warms, and reminds me, as though I could forget, that she is taking care of me.

Acknowledgments

· ·

All of the essays were commissioned specifically for *What My Mother Gave Me: Thirty-one Women on the Gifts That Mattered Most.*

"Heart's Desire" by Roxana Robinson. Copyright © 2012 Roxana Robinson. "Heart's Desire" originally appeared in *Narrative* magazine.

"The Missing Photograph" by Caroline Leavitt. Copyright © 2012 Caroline Leavitt.

"Mess Up Your Mind" by Maud Newton. Copyright © 2012 Maud Newton.

"My Disquieting Muse" by Jean Hanff Korelitz. Copyright © 2012 Jean Hanff Korelitz.

"The Unicorn Princess" by Katha Pollitt. Copyright © 2012 Katha Pollitt.

"White Christmas" by Ann Hood. Copyright © 2012 Ann Hood.

"My Mother's Armor" by Margo Jefferson. Copyright © 2012 Margo Jefferson.

"Three-Hour Tour" by Emma Straub. Copyright © 2012 Emma Straub. "Three-Hour Tour" appears in *Gulf Coast* 25.2.

"The Circle Line" by Mary Gordon. Copyright © 2012 Mary Gordon.

"The Gift Twice Given" by Judith Hillman Paterson. Copyright © 2012 Judith Hillman Paterson.

"The Last Happy Day of Her Life" by Cheryl Pearl Sucher. Copyright © 2012 Cheryl Pearl Sucher.

Contributors

. . . .

Elizabeth Benedict is a graduate of Barnard College and the author of five novels, including the best seller *Almost* and the National Book Award finalist *Slow Dancing*, as well as *The Joy of Writing Sex: A Guide for Fiction Writers*. She is the editor of the anthology *Mentors, Muses & Monsters: 30 Writers on the People Who Changed Their Lives*, and has written for the *New York Times, Boston Globe, Los Angeles Times, Esquire, Narrative Magazine, Allure, Salmagundi, Daedalus, Huffington Post*, the *Rumpus*, and *Tin House*. Her *Daedalus* essays, "What I Learned About Sex on the Internet" and "Murder One: Mad Dog Taborsky and Me," are Notable Essays in *Best American Essays* collections. She has taught widely and works as a writing coach and editor. Please visit www.elizabethbenedict.com.

Eleanor Clift is a contributor to *Newsweek* magazine and the *Daily Beast* website, and is a panelist on the public affairs show *The McLaughlin Group*. She has appeared as herself in several movies, including *Dave, Independence Day, Murder at 1600,* and in the CBS television series *Murphy Brown.* www.eleanor clift.com.

Lillian Daniel is the senior minister of the First Congregational Church, UCC, of Glen Ellyn, and author of *Tell It Like It Is: Reclaiming the Practice of Testimony,* which is the story of one church's attempt to get mainline Protestants to talk to each other about God. Her newest book, *This Odd and Wondrous Calling: The Public and Private Lives of Two Ministers,* coauthored by Martin B. Copenhaver, is a humorous and honest look at the ministry. Lillian also hosts the Chicago-based public television program *30 Good Minutes.* An editor at large for the *Christian Century* and a contributing editor at *Leadership Journal,* her work has also appeared in the *Huffington Post, Christianity Today, Leadership Journal, Books and Culture,* the *Journal for Preachers,* and in the daily e-mail devotionals available at ucc.org, with over twenty thousand subscribers. She has taught preaching at Yale Divinity School, Chicago Theological Seminary, and the University of Chicago Divinity School. A frequent speaker around the country, Lillian has preached at the National Cathedral, Duke Chapel, the Festival of Homiletics, King's College London, and Queen's University, Ontario.

Former U.S. Poet Laureate **Rita Dove** is the author of nine poetry books, a collection of short stories, and a novel. Her play *The Darker Face of the Earth* was produced at the Kennedy Center in Washington and the Royal National Theatre in London, among numerous other venues. *Sonata Mulattica,* her most recent poetry book, was published by W. W. Norton in 2009. *The Penguin Anthology of Twentieth-Century American Poetry,* released in 2011, was edited by Rita Dove. Her honors include the Pulitzer Prize in poetry, the National Humanities Medal, the Heinz Award, and the Fulbright Lifetime Achievement Medal. She is Commonwealth Professor of English at the University of Virginia and can be found on the Web at http://www.people.virginia.edu/~rfd4b/.

Mary Gordon is the author of seven novels, including *Final Payments, Spending,* and, most recently, *The Love of My Youth;* of two memoirs; of *The Stories of Mary Gordon,* winner of the Story Prize; of *Reading Jesus;* and of a biography of Joan of Arc. She is the recipient of a Lila Wallace–Reader's Digest Award, a Guggenheim Fellowship, and an Academy Award for Literature from the American Academy of Arts and Letters. She teaches at Barnard College.

Ann Hood is the author of nine novels, including the best sellers *The Red Thread, Somewhere Off the Coast of Maine,* and *The Knitting Circle,* as well as a collection of short stories, *An Ornithologist's Guide to Life,* and a memoir, *Comfort: A Journey Through Grief,* which was named by *Entertainment Weekly* as one of the top ten nonfiction books of 2008, and was a *New*

York Times Editor's Choice. Her new novel, *The Obituary Writer,* will be published in 2013.

Margo Jefferson is a Pulitzer Prize–winning cultural critic. Her book, *On Michael Jackson,* was published in 2006. She was a staff writer for the *New York Times* for twelve years, and has contributed reviews and essays to *Bookforum,* the *Washington Post, New York Magazine,* and other publications. Her work has appeared in the anthologies *The Inevitable: Contemporary Writers Confront Death* (Norton), *Best African American Essays 2010* (Ballantine/One World), *Black Cool: One Thousand Streams of Blackness* (Counterpoint), and *The Mrs. Dalloway Reader* (Harcourt). She has also written and performed a solo theater piece, *Sixty Minutes in Negroland.*

Karen Karbo is the author of three novels and a memoir, all of which were named *New York Times* Notable Books of the Year. Her 2003 memoir, *The Stuff of Life,* about the last year she spent with her father before his death, was a *New York Times* Notable Book, a *People Magazine* Critics' Choice, a Books for a Better Life Award finalist, and a winner of the Oregon Book Award for Creative Nonfiction. Her short stories, essays, articles, and reviews have appeared in *Elle, Vogue, Esquire, Outside,* the *New York Times, Salon,* and other magazines. Her most recent book is *How Georgia Became O'Keeffe: Lessons on the Art of Living,* the third in what she calls her Kick Ass Women trilogy.

Sheila Kohler is the author of nine novels, most recently *Becoming Jane Eyre* (2009), *Love Child* (2011), and *Bay of the Foxes* (2012), and three collections of short stories. Kohler has been awarded the O. Henry twice Award (1988, 2008), the Open Voice Award (1991), the Smart Family Foundation Prize (October 2000), the Willa Cather Prize judged by William Gass for *One Girl,* and the *Antioch Review* Prize (2004).

Her work has been translated and published widely abroad by Gallimard, France; Klett-Cotta, Germany; Shinchosha, Japan; Distribuidora Rekord, Brazil; Querido, Holland; Jonathan Cape and Bloomsbury in England; Penguin India; and will appear in Hungarian, Hebrew, Korean, and Chinese.

She has taught creative writing at City College, the Chenango Valley Conference at Colgate, Sarah Lawrence, The New School, SUNY Purchase, the West Side YMCA; in Montolieu, France; and at Columbia University and Brooklyn College. She now teaches at Princeton and Bennington.

Her novel *Cracks* has been filmed with Jordan Scott as director, Ridley Scott as executive producer, and Eva Green playing Miss G.

Jean Hanff Korelitz is the author of four novels (*Admission, The White Rose, The Sabbathday River,* and *A Jury of Her Peers*), a collection of poetry (*The Properties of Breath*), and a novel for children (*Interference Powder*). She has contributed essays and articles to several anthologies and many magazines, including *Vogue, Real Simple, Reader's Digest, More,* and *Newsweek.*

She lives in New Jersey with her family and has not seen a Woody Allen film in twenty years.

Caroline Leavitt is the *New York Times* best-selling author of *Pictures of You* and eight other novels. A book critic for *People* and the *Boston Globe,* she is a senior writing instructor for UCLA Writers' Program online, and she lives with her husband, the writer Jeff Tamarkin, and their son Max, in Hoboken, New Jersey. She can be found at www.caroline leavitt.com. Her new novel, *Is This Tomorrow,* will be published in the spring of 2013.

Elinor Lipman is the author of nine novels, including *Then She Found Me, The Inn at Lake Devine,* and, most recently, *The Family Man.* Her next, *The View from Penthouse B,* will be published in 2013, along with an essay collection. She recently held the Elizabeth Drew Chair in Creative Writing at Smith College.

Dahlia Lithwick is a senior editor at *Slate,* and in that capacity, writes the "Supreme Court Dispatches" and "Jurisprudence" columns. Her work has appeared in the *New York Times, Harper's,* the *Washington Post,* and *Commentary,* among other places. She received the Online News Association's award for online commentary in 2001 and again in 2005. She was editor of *The Best American Legal Writing of 2009.* She is the coauthor of *Me v. Everybody: Absurd Contracts* *for an Absurd World*, a legal humor book, and *I Will Sing Life: Voices from the Hole in the Wall Gang Camp*, a book about seven children from Paul Newman's camp with life-threatening illnesses. She appears frequently on television and radio, including *The Rachel Maddow Show* and *The Colbert Report*, and is a frequent guest on NPR.

Martha McPhee is the author of four novels, most recently *Dear Money*. Her work has been nominated for a National Book Award and honored by grants from the NEA and the Guggenheim Foundation. Please visit marthamcphee.com.

Mameve Medwed (named for two grandmothers, Mamie and Eva) is the author of the novels *Mail, Host Family, The End of an Error, How Elizabeth Barrett Browning Saved My Life* (2007 Massachusetts Book Award's Fiction Honor), and *Of Men and Their Mothers*. Her stories, essays, and book reviews have appeared in, among others, the *New York Times, Gourmet, Boston Globe*, the *Missouri Review, Newsday*, and the *Washington Post*. Born in Bangor, Maine (and claiming the title: "Bangor's other novelist"), she and her husband have two grown sons and live in Cambridge, Massachusetts. She has recently finished a memoir of an editorial friendship and is at work on a new novel. Her website is www.mamevemedwed.com.

Mary Morris is the author of fourteen books—six novels, including *Revenge*, three collections of short stories, and four

travel memoirs, including most recently *The River Queen*.
Her numerous short stories and travel essays have appeared
in such places as the *Atlantic, Narrative Magazine,* the *New
York Times,* and *Travel and Leisure.* The recipient of the
Rome Prize, Morris teaches writing at Sarah Lawrence College. For more information, visit her website, www.mary-
morris.net.

Cecilia Muñoz has been an activist for Latinos, immigrants,
and civil rights for twenty-five years, twenty of them at the
National Council of La Raza, where she directed the public
policy office. She is the recipient of a MacArthur Fellowship for her efforts, as well as numerous other awards. The
daughter of immigrants from Bolivia, she lives outside of
Washington, D.C., with her husband and two daughters.

Maud Newton received the 2009 Narrative Prize for an
excerpt from her novel-in-progress. She has written for the
New York Times Magazine, Narrative Magazine, the *Paris
Review Daily,* the *Los Angeles Times, Granta,* the *New York
Times Book Review,* the *Boston Globe,* the *Awl,* and many
other publications. Her blog, maudnewton.com, which con-
centrates on books, culture, politics, and other matters, has
been praised, cited, and criticized in the *New York Times,
Washington Post, Wall Street Journal,* the *Times* (UK), *Forbes,
New York Magazine, Entertainment Weekly, USA Today,* the
UK *Telegraph,* the *New Yorker, Poets & Writers, Slate,* and

the *San Francisco Chronicle,* among other periodicals. She has more than 130,000 followers on Twitter.

Joyce Carol Oates is the author most recently of the memoir *A Widow's Story* and the story collection *Sourland.* She is Professor of the Arts at Princeton University and has been a member, since 1978, of the American Academy of Arts and Letters.

Judith Hillman Paterson is a graduate of Hollins College and Auburn University. She is the author of four books, including her critically acclaimed childhood memoir, *Sweet Mystery: A Book of Remembering* (FSG/Univ. of Alabama Press). Her essays and book reviews have appeared in *Vogue, Ms.,* the *Village Voice,* the *New York Times,* the *Chicago Tribune,* the Baltimore *Evening Sun,* the *Atlanta Journal-Constitution,* and the *Washington Post.* She is working on a historical novel set in Alabama, from the coming of cotton through the civil rights movement. She lives and writes beside a lake in North Carolina.

Marge Piercy (www.margepiercy.com) is the author of seventeen novels, most recently *Sex Wars,* and of eighteen volumes of poetry, most recently *The Hunger Moon: New and Selected Poems 1980–2010* (Knopf). She has written two nonfiction books and a memoir, *Sleeping with Cats* (HarperCollins Perennial). A CD of political poetry is available online—*Louder: We Can't Hear You (Yet!).* Her work has been translated into nineteen languages. She has given readings, lectures, and workshops at well over four hundred venues.

Abigail Pogrebin, a former *60 Minutes* producer, is the author of *Stars of David: Prominent Jews Talk About Being Jewish* and *One and the Same: My Life as an Identical Twin and What I've Learned About Everyone's Struggle to Be Singular*. Her best-selling Amazon Kindle Single, "Showstopper," chronicles her teenage adventures in the original Broadway cast of a Stephen Sondheim flop, *Merrily We Roll Along*. She has written for numerous publications including *New York Magazine, Harper's Bazaar,* the *Daily Beast, Salon, Tablet,* and the *Huffington Post,* and she moderates the interview series "What Everyone's Talking About" at The JCC in Manhattan. She lives in Manhattan with her husband and two children.

Katha Pollitt is a poet, essayist, and columnist for the *Nation*. She is the author of six books, most recently *Learning to Drive,* a collection of personal essays, and *The Mind-Body Problem,* a collection of poems. She has won many awards and prizes for her work, including Guggenheim and Whiting fellowships, two National Magazine Awards, a National Book Critics Circle Award in poetry, and an American Book Award for lifetime achievement. She lives in New York City with her husband, Steven Lukes, and is the mother of Sophie Pollitt-Cohen.

Luanne Rice is the author of thirty novels, including *Little Night* (Viking/Pamela Dorman Books). Five of her books have been made into movies and miniseries, twenty-two have been consecutive *New York Times* best sellers, and two of her pieces have been featured in off-Broadway theater productions. She divides her time between New York City and Old Lyme, Connecticut.

Roxana Robinson is most recently the author of the novel *Cost,* which was named one of the five best fiction books of 2008 by the *Washington Post,* and won the Maine Writers and Publishers Alliance Award for Fiction. She is also the author of the novels *Sweetwater, This Is My Daughter,* and *Summer Light;* three story collections; and the biography *Georgia O'Keeffe: A Life.* Four of these were *New York Times* Notable Books. Robinson's work has appeared in the *New Yorker,* the *Atlantic, Harper's, Best American Short Stories,* and elsewhere. She was named a Literary Lion by the New York Public Library, and has received fellowships from the NEA, the MacDowell Colony, and the Guggenheim Foundation. She lives in New York City.

Elissa Schappell is the author of two books of fiction, most recently *Blueprints for Building Better Girls,* and *Use Me,* which was a finalist for the PEN/Hemingway Award, a *New York Times* Notable Book and a *Los Angeles Times* Best Book of the Year, and she is coeditor with Jenny Offill of two anthologies of essays, *The Friend Who Got Away* and *Money Changes Everything.* She is currently a contributing editor at *Vanity Fair,* a founding editor and now editor at large of *Tin House,* and a former senior editor of the *Paris Review*. Her short stories, nonfiction, book reviews, and essays have appeared in such places as the *Paris Review*, the *New York Times Book Review*, *Bomb*, *Vogue*, *Spin*, *One Story*, and anthologies, including *The KGB Bar Reader*, *The Bitch in the House*, *Sex and Sensibility*, and *The Mrs. Dalloway Reader*. She currently teaches at NYU and the Low-Residency MFA program at Queens University in Charlotte, North Carolina. She lives in Brooklyn with her family.

Lisa See is the author of several *New York Times* best sellers, including *Dreams of Joy*, *Shanghai Girls*, *Peony in Love*, and *Snow Flower and the Secret Fan*. Her novels have been published in thirty-nine languages. Her next novel, *China Dolls*, will be published by Random House in the spring of 2013.

Charlotte Silver is the author of the best seller *Charlotte au Chocolat: Memories of a Restaurant Girlhood*. Her second book, a young adult novel called *The Chaperone*, is forthcoming from Roaring Brook Press. She grew up in Harvard Square before attending Bennington College. She studied writing at The Bread Loaf Writers' Conference, and has been published in the *New York Times*. She lives in New York.

Susan Stamberg is a founding mother of National Public Radio, and the first woman to anchor a nightly national network news program (NPR's *All Things Considered*). A Fellow of the American Academy of Arts and Sciences, she is author of two books, and editor of a third. Her mother was Anne Rosalind Rosenberg Levitt. Her husband was Louis Collins Stamberg. Their son is the actor Josh Stamberg.

Emma Straub is the author of *Laura Lamont's Life in Pictures* and *Other People We Married*. Her fiction and essays have appeared in *Tin House, Slate,* the *Paris Review Daily, Cousin Corrine's Reminder,* and many other journals. She lives with her husband in Brooklyn, New York, which is only a forty-five-minute subway ride away from her mother. More information can be found at www.emmastraub.net.

Cheryl Pearl Sucher is an award-winning American journalist, essayist, reviewer, and fiction writer who lives with her Kiwi husband in Hawkes Bay, New Zealand. Her first novel, *The Rescue of Memory,* was published by Scribner in hardcover and as a Berkley Signature Series paperback. Her writing has recently appeared in the *Bellevue Literary Review,* the *Southwest Review,* and *Huffington Post.* "Ka Hau E Wha: The Southernmost Jewish Community in the World," her contribution to the forthcoming *Jewish Lives in New Zealand,* was published by Random House New Zealand in March 2012. She is currently completing her second novel, *Lost Cities.*